A Blueprint
of His Dissent

A Blueprint
of His Dissent

Madness and Method in Tennyson's Poetry

Roger S. Platizky

Lewisburg
Bucknell University Press
London and Toronto: Associated University Presses

Associated University Presses
440 Forsgate Drive
Cranbury, NJ 08512

Associated University Presses
25 Sicilian Avenue
London WC1A 2QH, England

Associated University Presses
P.O. Box 488, Port Credit
Mississauga, Ontario
Canada L5G 4M2

The paper used in this publication meets the requirements of the American National Standard for Permanence of Paper for Printed Library Materials Z39.48-1984.

Library of Congress Cataloging-in-Publication Data

Platizky, Roger S., 1953–
   A blueprint of his dissent.

   Bibliography: p.
   Includes index.
   1. Tennyson, Alfred Tennyson, Baron, 1809–1892—
Knowledge—Psychology.   2. Mental illness in literature.
3. Psychology in literature.   I. Title.
PR5592.P74P57   1989   821'.8   87-46433
ISBN 0-8387-5151-2 (alk. paper)

PRINTED IN THE UNITED STATES OF AMERICA

This book is dedicated in loving memory to
my grandmother,
Celia Herzig.

Contents

Acknowledgments

The writing of this book involved the positive engagement between the self and many significant others in the form of intellectual challenges and moral support. For the former, I am especially indebted to Daniel A. Harris, the director of my dissertation. I would also like to thank Barry Qualls and William Walling for reading and commenting on an earlier version of this manuscript. Other people who provided valuable moral support, guidance, computer skills, and inspiration as I expanded and reworked the manuscript are Luz María Umpierre, Susan Swartzlander, Virginia Hyman, Linda Schulze, Jeffrey Feld, Tod Bergman, Tony D'Augelli, and Marion Gindes. Finally, it is with deepest appreciation that I thank my family—Adeline, Ben, Andrew, Charlene, Selma, Mark, Isaac, and Samuel—for having faith in me. This book is for all of you.

Portions of this study appeared in shorter form as journal articles:
"The Watcher on the Column: Religious Enthusiasm and Madness in Tennyson's 'St. Simeon Stylites.'" *Victorian Poetry* 25 (Summer 1987): 181–87. Copyright 1987 by West Virginia University. Reprinted by permission.

"Tennyson's Rizpah: Mother of Sorrows or Mother Devourer?" *Literature and Psychology* 33 (1987): 62–69. Copyright 1987 by *Literature and Psychology*.

Permission has been granted by Gale Research Company for the use of the etching of St. Simeon Stylites on the cover of the book. The etching can be found in William Hone, *The Everyday Book; or, A Guide to the Year*, Gale Research, 1976; originally published by William Tegg, 1827.

Introduction

The moment when, together, the work of art and madness are born and fulfilled is the beginning of the time when the world finds itself arraigned by that work of art and responsible before it for what it is.

—Michel Foucault, *Madness and Civilization*

Aside from the critical reception of *Maud*, there has been relatively little scholarly debate or detailed analysis of poetry by Tennyson that deals with the theme and social implications of madness. There has been even less discussion of Tennyson's marked ability to sustain a level of psychological complexity in poems that span his lifetime and deal with the subject of madness in an organized, innovative, dynamic, and culturally informative manner. In recent years, progress has been made in this area by writers like Robert Bernard Martin (*Tennyson: The Unquiet Heart*) and Ann C. Colley (*Tennyson and Madness*). Following in the footsteps of Harold Nicolson (*Tennyson: Aspects of His Life Character and Poetry*), E. D. H. Johnson (*The Alien Vision of Victorian Poetry*), Ralph Wilson Rader (*Tennyson's Maud: The Biographical Genesis*), Roy P. Basler (*Sex, Symbolism, and Psychology in Literature*), and Charles Tennyson and Hope Dyson (*The Tennysons: Background to Genius*),[1] Martin and Colley have adduced biographical and historical evidence to show how Tennyson's poetry was informed by his literary and personal knowledge of mental pathology—his fear of the "black blood" of his family, his neurotic hypersensitivity to criticism, his hypochondria and resort to hydropathic institutions, and his extensive readings in works ranging from Burton's *Anatomy of Melancholy* and Shakespeare's *Hamlet* and *King Lear* to psychiatric texts of his period by John Haslam, George Man Burrows, Philippe Pinel, and Matthew Allen (with whom Tennyson formed a business partnership), among others. The focus of these critical works, however, has been primarily biographical or historical rather than closely textual; that is, we learn more about the psychology of Tennyson himself at a particular moment than we do about how the language of the poetry itself reveals psychological patterns and tensions that are timely as well as historical, socially conscious as well as aesthetically distanced. It is with the language of the poetry that my study is concerned.

In the chapters that follow, I have explored the variety of methods Tennyson uses to make the language of his poetry on madness psychologically dynamic, and on whether his characterizations of madness indicate a view of derangement that is conservative (i.e., culturally normative) or more subversive (i.e., critical of cultural norms) than is generally thought. To illustrate this study, I have focused on five poems—"St. Simeon Stylites" (1833), Maud (1855), "Lucretius" (1868), "Rizpah" (1880), and "Romney's Remorse" (1889). While other poems with mad themes certainly could have been central—for instance, "Mariana," "The Lady of Shalott," or Idylls of the King—I have selected these because they span the poet's lifetime, yet have never been studied collectively; because they show that Tennyson's interest in madness extends to male representations as well as female, and that he could delineate both realistically; and because the poems draw on alienated speakers whose madness arises not primarily from their own monomania or from Romantic self-enclosure[2] but, rather, from problematic Victorian conflicts about faith, love, death, and animality. Taken as a group, these poems show, furthermore, that Maud was hardly a fluke and that Tennyson possessed a keen and sometimes countercultural awareness of abnormal psychology in an age that was reinvestigating the causes, manifestations, possible cures, and cultural determinants of madness.

Historically, Tennyson's treatment of madness in these poems is influenced by the nineteenth century's relatively tolerant but still apprehensive attitude toward the insane. As writers like Michel Foucault and, more recently, Andrew Scull have demonstrated,[3] the Victorian view, image, and treatment of the insane were markedly different from that of the eighteenth century. The Age of Reason predominantly (Johnson and Smart are exceptions) regarded the deranged as beasts and as sinners who, being punished with madness, were to be beaten into submission (cf. "Rizpah," 45–50) and put on public display. The Romantics, especially Wordsworth, helped to humanize madness in poetry, and the Victorians, although they feared derangement, generally ceased to regard madness in terms of moral absolutes and divine imperatives. In addition, they were responsible for converting madhouses into rehabilitative asylums, in the belief that the insane were not subhuman and could once again be made productive to society. This was because their disturbances were mostly the result of nervous disorders that were scientifically identifiable. At the same time, however, that they were progressive in their treatment of the insane, the Victorians promulgated their own myths

about madness and sexuality[4] and sanctioned the very kinds of repression and renunciation of instinctive desire that could lead to the
development of hypertrophied consciences in the less stable, who
would needlessly assume guilt if they could not measure up to
cultural, as well as personal, expectations. This paradoxical attitude
toward madness is reflected in Tennyson's poems on the subject. In
each of the poems under discussion, there is a tension between
individual trust and social expectations that can be seen in the psychological dynamic between the nonconforming self (the hyper-vig-
ilant, mad speaker) and the socialized "other"—the silent auditor(s),
who is (are) perceived as more powerful than the self.

To dramatize this conflict between the self and the other and to
create a closed-in world of "centrality"[5] and surveillance, Tennyson
uses the forms of the dramatic monologue and the monody (for
Maud) in psychologically innovative ways. In each poem, the speaker
seeks some form of pacification and approbation from the silent
auditor(s). Although Robert Langbaum in his classic work on the
dramatic monologue, *The Poetry of Experience*, regards the auditors
as "pragmatic constructions" that "derive their life from the speaker"
and through which "the speakers reveal themselves,"[6] the silent lis-
teners may serve a psychological as well as a dramatic function. As
Dorothy Mermin argues, the auditors "have power too," because the
"speaker's utterance defines itself in terms of the auditor, whose
presence thus creates the possibility that the speaker might not be able
to speak."[7] Moreover, in these five works by Tennyson, the auditors
are what Sartre would call "reflectors," in that the other is seen as
withholding the self.[8] Each of the five speakers feels either incomplete
or threatened by the possible disapproval and punishment of the
other: St. Simeon Stylites needs the validation of a speechless God to
prove that his masochistic austerities have meant something; Lucretius, who cannot accept the "twy-nature" of the self, projects it
onto satyrs and hetairai that both threaten and mirror the self; the
speaker of *Maud*, a social outcast and orphan, seeks narcissistic union
with Maud; Romney needs Mary Abbot's approval to feel he is saved
from hell's fire; Rizpah fuses her identity with that of her dead son
Willy because she has no purpose to live without him. Furthermore,
fear that the other will not complete, rescue, or forgive the self is
implied when Simeon believes he will be abandoned by his God, the
narrator of *Maud* fears he will become victimized by Maud's predatory nature, and Romney wonders whether Mary is poisoning
rather than curing him with her "dark opiate." According to Lacan,
these paranoid reactions on the part of the speakers toward the silent
others would result from the speakers' narcissistic efforts to appropri-

ate the self in the other.[9] Since the appropriated other is supposed to complete or "mirror" the self, a paranoid reaction occurs when the idealized self—Simeon's angel with the "glittering face," Lucretius's Lucretia, Romney's Mary, Rizpah's Willy, and the protagonist's Maud—cannot (will not) confirm the ego's ideal. When this occurs, the punishing conscience of the instinctively aggressive speaker gains preeminence: Simeon fears that he is unclean and will not be saved, Lucretius is oppressed by nightmares of incubi, Romney hears the critics jeering at him in hell, Rizpah remembers her helplessness at the execution of her son, and the protagonist of *Maud* torments himself with thoughts of his cowardliness. Furthermore, the speakers' symbiotic dependence on forces outside of themselves for validation contributes to their neurotic vacillations in self-esteem and to their inconsolable feelings of alienation.

Although alienation, paranoia, and neurotic vacillations in self-esteem may all seem like twentieth-century conceptions, their roots run deep in history and literature: the ancient Greeks deal with the theme of alienation and madness in such works as *Ajax* and *Oedipus Rex,* the pathology of paranoia was well established by the midnineteenth century,[10] and the kinds of mood swings that today we would call neurotic or manic-depressive, were accessible to Tennyson from such works as *Hamlet* and *The Anatomy of Melancholy.* Also available to Tennyson were contemporary case studies and descriptions of hallucinations, lucid intervals, somatic derangement, inherited madness, and the *idée fixe*—all of which are represented in these five poems. Since our own understanding of mental pathology springs from similar historical roots, we strengthen rather than damage those roots by using modern psychological tools of interpretation. In this way, the contemporaneity of Tennyson's poems is respected without miring them in the past. The theme of madness creates the need for a bridge between the past and present, because the subject involves a timeless concern with human behavior and human conflict that is indigenous, as art reveals, in the kinds of societies—the Victorian as well as our own—that could press people to venture beyond the well-lit borders of conformity and reason.

A Blueprint
of His Dissent

1

"Hidden Wells of Scorching Fire"
The Emerging Pattern

And men, whose reason long was blind,
From cells of madness unconfined,
Oft lose whole years of darker mind.
                                    —Tennyson, "The Two Voices"

Tennyson laid the groundwork for his poetry on madness early when at fourteen, he precociously composed the three-act, seventeen-hundred-line play *The Devil and the Lady* (1823–24). Crossing Elizabethan stichomythia with Jonsonian ribaldry, the play satirizes, among other things, the duplicity of appearances and the pomposity of professionals. In the second act, Tennyson uses the "damning license of a repartee"[1] to mock Pharmaceutus for diagnosing Antonio, the wittiest of Amoret's suitors, as a "hypochondriac or hysterical" (2.4.98). Pharmaceutus bases his diagnosis on Antonio's wrath: his clenched fist, the "wild glance of [his] tumultuous eyes," and the "broken interrupted words" (2.4.132–35). The apothecary recommends that Antonio be "blooded" (2.4.47), a method still occasionally employed in Tennyson's time to treat symptoms such as those described. Tennyson scorns Pharmaceutus, whom even the Devil calls "a mad, drug-dealing, vile apothecary" (2.3.34), for his judgments based on appearance and his pedantic panaceas when he gives the cynical Antonio the stronger reply:

> Why! thou dead idiot, wouldst thou thus behave
> As I were mad? In trust and faith I were so
> If I should bear with thee. I should deserve
> Commission of lunacy preferred against me. . . .
>
> (2.4.122–25)

From this piece of juvenilia, it is apparent that even the young Tennyson liked experimenting with the potential of the theatrical utterance, the ways that language could be self-inflating or -deflating, bombastic or stressful, imperative or questioning, accusational or

17

defensive. This fascination with language and with the possibilities of repartee would gradually carry over and be transformed into Tennyson's dramatic monologues on madness. In the dramatic monologue, the "damning license of a repartee" between two characters in works like *The Devil and the Lady* would become the private, internalized battle—a kind of psychic repartee—between two sides (one usually damning, the other glorifying) of a mad speaker's consciousness. The "damning license" of such internal colloquies would be the ability of the utterance both to liberate and ensnare the speakers as they revealed their divided selves through language. The Pharmaceutus character would gradually evolve into the silent auditor of the dramatic monologue, a kind of social mediator for whom the alienated monologist develops a kind of love-hate, passive-aggressive dependency relationship. The tone of the monologists, while retaining its original theatricality, would alter in one important respect: after writing *The Devil and the Lady,* Tennyson never again would treat the subject of madness in a purely satirical, Punch-and-Judy manner. The conflicts would become more serious, the imagery more haunting, the tone more poignant, and the characterizations more dimensional.

While there may be various contributing causes for this change, the mental breakdown of Tennyson's father in 1824[2] and his death after subsequent bouts of dementia in 1831 would have been sufficient reason for Tennyson to alter his representations of madness in subsequent poems. The influence that the father had on Tennyson, as well as on the rest of the family, was formidable. As Diana Basham records, the father's "hypochondria and mental miseries were broadcast among his children." Tennyson and his father were "so psychically close" that they both suffered repeatedly from similar psychosomatic symptoms, including the terror of going blind.[3] Furthermore, Tennyson's brothers Edward, Septimus, Frederick, and Charles and his sisters Mary, Cecilia, and Matilda all suffered from emotional disturbances which, like Tennyson, they feared they had inherited from their father's bloodline.[4] For Alfred, who was to become the most successful and famous of the Tennyson's, the father's influence had a double edge. It was, after all, Tennyson's father who had first recognized his son's talent and encouraged him to write poetry, the career choice that would shape his destiny and make him the most celebrated poet in Victorian England. It was also, however, the father whose illnesses and violence against loved ones—once in a fit of dementia, he threatened to stab his son Frederick "in the jugular vein and in the heart" with a large knife[5]—led to an emotionally unstable household. Furthermore, it was the father's despondency and debt (later alluded to in *Maud*) that would compel Tennyson to leave Cambridge without taking his degree.[6] Ambivalent feelings toward such a father, who could be both pitied and judged, loved and feared, were a likely response. Such feelings helped to shape the new way in which Tennyson would begin to characterize and express madness in his poetry.

In comparing the imagery of a group of early works, like *The Devil and the Lady,* "Armageddon" (1828), "The Coach of Death" (1828), and "Remorse" (1827), with that of a group of later ones, "St. Simeon Stylites" (1833), *Maud* (1855), "Lucretius" (1868), and "Romney's Remorse" (1889), we see a pattern emerging that depends on the assumed power or helplessness of the poetic personae. That is, we see how imagination empowers those speakers who feel either protected or vitalized by forces in the universe, while it frequently torments the maddened speakers who feel that control might be taken away at any time by some threatening or depriving other. For instance, in the unstable world of Simeon Stylites, Abaddon and Asmodeus, who are comically viewed as pranksters of the Devil in *The Devil and the Lady* (2.7.27–30), become tormenting demons who swarm against the isolated pillar saint in his guilt-ridden sleep (166–75). The image changes because Simeon is ridden through with doubt that his "pillar-punishment" has had any ultimate purpose. Similarly, whereas the visionary speaker of "Armageddon" marvels at a beatific "young seraph" with "inutterable shining eyes" (2:5) Simeon, who lacks this kind of trust in his own mystical powers, questions whether he actually sees an angel with a "glittering face," then tries deliriously to "draw, draw, draw" it into existence as a sign of his salvation (200–210). Unlike the visionary of "Armageddon" who revels in the glory that he sees, Simeon privatizes the imagery while feverishly vacillating between thinking he is damned by demons and saved by angels. Because his own sense of self is so fragmented, Simeon exists in a limbo between vision and hallucination, and the reader questions his sanity. There is also a preview in "Armageddon" of the unclean, half-human spirits that will later haunt the unstable speaker in "Lucretius." While the mystic of "Armageddon" can imaginatively pass from these "ill-omened things" (1:53) to the vision of the luminous seraph, Lucretius cannot fling from his consciousness the satyr, hetairai, or other unclean spirits that his imagination conjures. In comparing these sets of images, we see how traditional moral typologies in the earlier poems become psychologized in the later ones, as the symbols of good and evil get transformed in St. Simeon's and Lucretius's subconscious into judgmental others that punish or reward.

In "The Coach of Death" and "Remorse," two poems about the fear of death and the Last Judgment, a threatening otherness is represented by images of guilt and punishments of Hell—images that reoccur later in *Maud* (1855) and in "Romney's Remorse" (1889). Analogous to the way the hero of *Maud* remembers with hallucinatory guilt "the red-ribbed ledges [that] drip with a silent horror of blood" (3), the landscape in "The Coach of Death" also records horrors of the past:

> Thick sobs and short shrill screams arise
>   Along the sunless waste,
> And the things of past days with their horrible eyes
>   Look out from the cloudy vast.
>
>   (16–20)

The personified guilt of "horrible eyes" transferred to this landscape and that of "red-ribbed ledges" to the landscape of *Maud* are examples of the "power of memory to ensnare an individual in his obsessions," which, as Ann Colley writes, "Belongs to nineteenth-century theories of madness."[7] As in all of Tennyson's poems on madness, settings are shaped, colored, and deformed (through transfer of effects) by the intensifying moods of the speaker. The primary difference between these two poetic settings is that the universal landscape of allegorical fear, which is controlled and solemnized with even rhymes in "The Coach of Death," becomes the psychic landscape of individual torment that is conveyed by the manic, irregularly rhymed lines of *Maud*. Imagery alters in a similar way from the early, allegorical poem "Remorse" to the late dramatic monologue "Romney's Remorse." In the first poem, an unnamed, universal figure anxiously awaits the Last Judgment. Because of his deep shame and guilt, he vividly imagines the punishment that awaits him in hell (50–52) and wonders how he will "bear the withering look / Of men and angels" when he dies (81–82). Equally threatened by the punishments of hell, the more passive-aggressive portraitist Romney imagines hell inhabited by sinners worse than himself who resemble the critics that jeered at his art on earth (127–34). Thus, while the Everyman of "Remorse" can only, with allegorical rigidity, confess his sins and dread a morally predictable judgment, Romney is afforded the "damning license of a repartee" to vacillate in his opiate-induced delirium between feeling that he will be saved by his angelic wife, Mary Abbot, or damned because he abandoned her for the harlot, Art (110).

This kind of dependency relationship between the self and some idealized other, like Mary Abbot or Maud, from whom the self seeks validation, is the most consistent conflict that the dramatic monologues on madness and their precursors share. Tennyson first explores the dependency relationship in early love poems like "Mariana" (1830), "Fatima" (1832), "Oenone" (1832), "The Lover's Tale" (1832), and "The Lady of Shalott" (1832). In each of these poems, an unrequited, betrayed, or desired love leads to a narcissistic attachment to a distant or depriving other, who becomes the speaker's *idée fixe*—another hallmark of Tennyson's poems on madness. The reaction of each speaker, however, to the missing lover varies from paralyzing despondency to idolatrous aggressiveness. Narcissistic love is the pleasure principle's drive to complete the self through the other, who becomes a mirror of self-worth. As Freud states in *Civilization and its Discontents*, the danger of such a relationship "is that we are never so defenseless against suffering as when we love, never so helplessly unhappy as when we have lost our loved object or its love."[8] In response to such loss, Mariana imprisons herself in her own mindscape and somnolent refrain, "I am aweary, aweary, / I would that I were dead!"; Fatima passionately vows that she *"will possess* [her lover] or will die" (39); the passive-aggressive Oenone warns that she will "Talk with the wild Cassandra" (259) in her burning, vengeful love for the betraying Paris; Julian hallucinates about Camilla until he is able to fling "Her empty phantom" from him in a whirlwind fantasy that mixes repressed rage and heroism (2 : 187–205).[9] Finally, in "The Lady of Shalott," the ultimate emblem of narcissistic attachment, the woman's mirror cracking "from side to side" (115) as she seeks new identity through Lancelot, foreshadows the heroine's death, her sacrifice to a consuming passion.

Clearly, the idolatrous relationships in these early love poems forecast the kinds of psychological dependencies we find later in poems like *Maud* and "Rizpah"; yet in the latter poems, the pathology of attachment becomes much more pronounced. While Julian and the hero of *Maud* both worship their unrequited loves on the altars of their own minds, Julian questions his jealousy toward Camilla and her chosen lover, Lionel—"And why was I to darken their pure love . . . / Because my own was darkened? (1 : 715–17)—whereas the pathologically jealous and paranoid hero of *Maud* not only feels betrayed by Maud, but also envies and despises the "new-made lord" who has been chosen to marry her, views Maud's father as the personification of evil, and kills Maud's brother. Equally disturbing and self-reflexive is Rizpah's obsessive love for her son, Willy, who died publicly on the scaffold. The Liebestod theme that Tennyson employs in the early love poems alters radically in "Rizpah" as the lost love object becomes a deceased son rather than an absent lover and the *idée fixe* becomes the son's numbered bones, a point I will discuss more fully in the chapter "Rizpah: Mother of Sorrows or Mother Devourer?"

A final important pattern we see emerging in Tennyson's poetry on madness is his speakers' paranoid fear of incorporation by unclean spirits—actually repressed desires—that is most emphatically present in "Lucretius" but is also a potential source of menace in two early poems, "The Passions" (1832) and "Pierced through with knotted thorns of barren pain" (1832). The first four lines of "The Passions" could well have been an epigraph for "Lucretius":

> Beware, beware, ere thou takest
> The draught of misery!
> Beware, beware, ere thou wakest
> The scorpions that sleep in thee!

In "Lucretius," the "scorpions" that sleep in the subconscious of the Epicurean speaker are repressed desires that are guiltily awakened by Lucilia's love philter, and this "draught of misery" turns hidden desires into nightmarish phantasms, the punishing others of the speaker's own psyche. What happens to Lucretius recalls Schopenhauer's view, in *The World as Will and Representation* (1819), of the source of madness:

> . . . the will's opposition to let what is repellent to it come to the knowledge of the intellect is the spot through which insanity can break through into the spirit.[10]

We see this process also at work in Tennyson's most despondent early poem, "Pierced through with knotted thorns of barren pain." Bleak as Hopkins's dark sonnet "No Worse, There is None," Tennyson's poem depicts a consciousness at war with itself and terrified of what it has repressed—the "scummy sulphur seething far below" in the "chasms" of thought that exist underneath the "volcanic plain" of the mind (4–6). Like Lucretius, who dreams of "flaring atom-streams" (38) and breasts scorching him with flame (60–66), and Simeon Stylites, who recalls with anguish how "all hell beneath / Made me boil over" (167–68), the speaker of this early poem practices stillness and hyper-vigilance "For fear the hidden wells of scorching fire / Should spout between the clefts and shower flame" (9–11). In each case, the flames of passion burn so intensely because the speaker has tried so vigilantly to resist them. Instead of owning up to these passions, the speakers project them onto some other landscape or person, hence the paranoid reaction: the speaker becomes crazed that some unclean spirit or eerie landscape is about to swallow him.

The fear of psychic engulfment is a primal one, and that fear is intensified when one believes, as Tennyson did, in inherited madness. We see Tennyson's attempt to avoid incorporation of his father's black-bloodedness in "The Outcast" (1826), a poem that prefigures the ambivalent father-son relationship in *Maud* and serves as a contrast to the psychic bond between mother and son in "Rizpah." The conflict in "The Outcast" is the tension between the father's ubiquitous presence and Tennyson's attempt to resist that melancholy influence. This is a difficult task since nature's landscape (and the speaker's mind) is infused with memory of the father:

> Each broken stile, each wavy path,
> Each hollowed hawthorn, damp, and black,
> Each brook that chatters noisy wrath
> Among its knotted reeds, bring back
> Lone images of varied pain
> To this worn mind and fevered brain.
>
> (15–20)

Unlike the melancholy Mariana, whose thoughts are willed over to an absent lover and gloomy landscape, the speaker of this poem tries to maintain his ego boundaries by choosing not to pace his "Father's Hall" (21), for fear of "what Memory might recall" (29) if he did. Conversely, the heroes of *Maud* and Rizpah cross over that boundary, and discover madness on the other side. Their narcissistic need to merge with the "other" paradoxically leads to psychic fragmentation, for as R. D. Laing writes in *The Divided Self*, "a firm sense of one's own autonomous identity is required"; otherwise, "any and every relationship threatens the individual with loss of identity."[11] Clearly, neither the protagonist of *Maud* nor Rizpah has this firm sense of autonomous identity: the former is terrified of raging and dying as his suicidal father did (1:54–55), and the latter still feels the bones of her son moving in her side years after his death (53). In fact, as I hope the following chapters will amply demonstrate, the absence of this sense of autonomous identity, and the consequential dependence on others for self-valuation, is the common link between all of Tennyson's mad poems and characters.

As we can surmise from this survey of some of Tennyson's earliest poems, Tennyson may have had an earlier poem—its imagery, conflict, and theme—in mind as he composed his later poems on madness. Thus, we find features in common—the *idée fixe*, the narcissistic conflict between self and other, the transfer of effects, the fear of judgment and punishment, the problem of repressed guilt and desire, the absence of stable ego boundaries—as we move from early poems like "Remorse," "Fatima," and "Pierced through with knotted thorns of barren pain" to later ones, like "Rizpah" and "Romney's Remorse." The primary contrast we note is that while the earlier poems primarily use allegory (e.g., "Armageddon," "Remorse," "The Coach of Death," "The Passions"), satire (*The Devil and the Lady*), lyric (e.g., "The Outcast," "I Wander in Darkness and Sorrow"), and prosopopoeia (e.g., "Oenone," "Fatima") to dramatize the personal, moral, and psychological conflicts of the speakers, the later poems use the form of the dramatic monologue to explore more pathological states of mind and cultural, as well as personal, conflicts.

While critics have posited many theories about the formation of Tennyson's dramatic monologues,[12] the form itself, because of its alienated orators and silent auditors, provides an excellent vehicle for dramatizing the parapraxis of the disturbed speakers. Because the valuating audience is silent and the speakers lack firm ego boundaries, the speakers project their conflicts onto the other, analogous to the way a patient might abreact before a therapist upon whom he has transferred his conflict. The parapraxis is revealed through symptoms, stresses, and defense mechanisms, like Simeon's manic list of hypochondriacal complaints, the hero's hyper-vigilance in *Maud*, Lucretius's stammering before the gods, Romney's regressions, and Rizpah's *idée fixe*. In each case the parapraxis is a reaction to the tension of being watched, judged by silent witnesses within the claustrophobic worlds that the dramatic monologue and monody frame. That someone is listening but not responding brings tension to the surface that might otherwise be repressed, privatized, or more controlled (as in the earlier allegorical and lyrical poems). The auditors' presence gives the monologists the occasion to pour out their feelings; the auditors' silence stokes their guilt for, perhaps, saying too much. The form of the dramatic monologue also gave Tennyson the license to question and challenge several Victorian concerns— about faith, animality, love, and duty—that are at the root of his speakers' conflicts. These cultural determinants of madness will be examined in the ensuing chapters.

The following chapters on "St. Simeon Stylites," *Maud*, "Lucretius," "Rizpah," and "Romney's Remorse" analyze the variety of ways in which Tennyson dramatizes madness in poems that span fifty years, from the early to the late Victorian period. Whether Tennyson had a definite or even informal plan for the specific chronology of these poems is a matter of speculation. Poetic creation is often unpredictable—sometimes linear, sometimes regressive, sometimes commissioned, sometimes defiant. Pressures from critics, publishers, and accountants; the influences and competitions of other authors; and moments of self-doubt and inspiration are among the variables that make elusive the chronological relationships among these poems. Still, the patterns that recur in imagery, symptomatology, and theme (see table) suggest a method to these poems on madness, one that evolved organically, if not quite systematically. Thus, while we can say, for instance, that the language of "St. Simeon Stylites" derives from syntactical patterns in "Supposed Confessions of a Second-Rate Sensitive Mind" (1830), and that Simeon's psychic repartee has much in common with the dialogic tensions we find in "The Two Voices" (1833), we cannot say with assurance which poem marks the transition between the earlier poems in which Tennyson introduced the subject of madness and the later ones. The frequency and durability of these patterns, however, are testimony to Tennyson's lifelong interest in the subject of madness and his ability to find a variety of poetic modes in which to express that abiding interest over time.

Poems (1823–1833)

Poems	Psychological Motifs	Themes
The Devil and the Lady (1823–24)	—allusion to hypochondria and hysteria —relationship between wrath and madness —the extremes people will go to be the chosen lover	—the duplicity of appearances —the problem of love —the hypocrisy of professional and religious cant
"The Outcast" (1826)	—guilt over father —alienation —transfer of effects —power of memory to enslave —problem with ego boundaries —*idée fixe*: father's mournful presence	—empathy and alienation —inherited guilt
"I Wander in Darkness and Sorrow" (1827)	—melancholia —transfer of effects —the power of memory to enslave —alienation	—loss of love —man seeking empathy with nature
"The Passions" (1827)	—the power of repressed guilt and desire —threats of the subconscious —self-torment	—the battlefield of the mind: passion vs. restraint

"King Charles's Vision" (1827)	—premonitory nightmares —hallucinations —ghosts —self against other	—how the mighty will fall —the nature of guilt
"Remorse" (1827)	—guilt and shame —self-torment —hyper-vigilance —anticipatory grief —*idée fixe*: Last Judgment—punishment in Hell	—the fear of the Last Judgment —the nature of guilt
"The Grave of a Suicide" (1827)	—transfer of effects —allusions to depression, frenzy, and suicide	—guilt and loss
"Armageddon" (1828)	—religious typologies that will later evolve into archetypes of punishment (demons) and reward (angels)	—journey of the soul —the duality of good and evil in God's universe —man as a cross between angel and demon
"The Coach of Death" (1828)	—transfer of effects —guilt —fear of the Last Judgment —the power of memory to enslave	—journey of the soul —Last Judgment

Poems	Psychological Motifs	Themes
"Mariana" (1830)	—melancholia —narcissistic withdrawal —hallucination —alienation —self vs. other —problem with ego boundaries —*idée fixe*: abandonment by lover	—the problem of love and loss —the torment of dependency
"Supposed Confessions of a Second-Rate Sensitive Mind" (1830)	—a mind divided against itself —breaks in syntax that will characterize the way utterance is shaped in the dramatic monologues —*idée fixe*: innocence of the self before corruption	—tenuous relationship between man and God —how can one be saved? —religious hypocrisy
"The Lover's Tale" (1832)	—idolatry —narcissistic love —hallucinations —problem with ego boundaries —problem with the self and others —partial insanity —*idée fixe*: Camilla	—the problems of love —the search for the ideal —the torment of dependency
"The Lady of Shalott" (1832)	—magic or madness? —problem with self vs. other —*Liebestod*: sacrificial love —*idée fixe*: Lancelot	—the problems of love —the conflict between choosing art and choosing life

Poem		
"Fatima" (1832)	—consuming passion —idolatry —narcissistic love —problem with ego boundaries —problem with self vs. other —*idée fixe:* absent lover	—the problem of love and unbridled desire —the torment of dependency
"Oenone" (1832)	—consuming passion —suicidal feelings —idolatry —repressed rage —problem between self and other —narcissistic love —*idée fixe:* Paris	—the problem of love: a woman scorned —the torment of dependency
"Pierced through with knotted thorns of barren pain" (1832)	—transfer of effects —power of repressed passions —despondency —fear of darker side of self —self-punishment	—dark night of the soul —the battlefield of the mind: passion vs. restraint
"The Two Voices" (1833)	—divided self —suicidal thoughts	—dialogue between the soul and the self
"St. Simeon Stylites" (1833)	—hypochondria —auditory hallucinations —repressed feelings of desire	—how can one be saved? —religious hypocrisy —men's terror of the silence of the

Poems	Psychological Motifs	Themes
	—problems between self and other —glorified self, hated self —*idée fixe*: the crown	gods

Later Dramatic Monologues
on Madness

Poems	Psychological Motifs	Themes
Maud (1855)	—hallucinations —hyper-vigilance —guilt over death of parents —ambivalence towards father —fear of inherited madness —paranoia —narcissistic love —spleen —incest anxiety —problem with ego boundaries —problem between the self and other —*idée fixe*: Maud and the suicidal father	—the problem of love —the personal and social causes and manifestations of madness —inherited madness —filial and social duty —the search for the ideal
"Lucretius" (1868)	—hyper-vigilance —self-punishing nightmares —hallucinations —threats of the subconscious	—the battlefield of the mind: passion vs. restraint —man's problem with accepting his animal nature —the nature of guilt

— partial insanity
— hated self, glorified self
— problem with ego boundaries
— sexual paranoia
— suicide
— *idée fixe:* hetairai, Helen's breasts

— the problem of accepting the death of a loved one
— social injustice and parental duty
— the nature of guilt
— the torment of dependency

"Rizpah" (1880)

— hallucinations
— narcissistic love
— paranoia
— hyper-vigilance
— problem with ego boundaries
— problem with self and other
— *idée fixe:* Willy's bones

"Romney's Remorse" (1889)

— hallucinations
— paranoia
— dread of Hell's punishment
— senility
— infantile dependency on other
— *idée fixe:* punishment of Hell, Mary's ring and her opiate

— duty to life or art?
— Last Judgment
— problem of love
— the nature of guilt
— the torment of dependency

2

"St. Simeon Stylites"
The Pillar and the Pillory

> How extremely difficult to level, with his real situation, the ideas
> of a man swelled up with morbid pride, solely intent on his high
> destinies, of thinking himself a privileged being, an emissary of
> heaven, a prophet from the Almighty, or even a divine personage.
> —Philippe Pinel, *A Treatise on Insanity* (1806)

In Tennyson's dramatic monologue "St. Simeon Stylites" (1833), the
distinctions between religious enthusiasm and insanity and between
vision and hallucination are pivotal ones. Yet these are distinctions
that critics have not explored largely as a result of relegating the theme
of madness in this poem to a minor role and viewing the speaker as a
religious hypocrite or demonic overreacher, worthy of scorn but little
sympathy.[1] The satire, while present, however, is not so overdone
that the reader is permitted merely to laugh at Simeon or become
hostile toward him. Although Tennyson's poem can be justly regarded as an indictment of the masochistic extremes of asceticism and
the pride that is paradoxically inherent in pious self-denial and mortification, Tennyson also humanizes Simeon and invests him with
cultural significance. He portrays Simeon as alienated, dying, and
deranged, and gives that derangement a Victorian context, for Simeon, though historically distanced, is a Victorian in disguise in his
anxieties about faith and animality.

Despite his saintly aspirations and manipulative aggression, Simeon
is driven not only by his own ambition, but also by cultural expectations and a religion of suffering prescribed by his God. In this
dramatic monologue, the pillar saint searches frantically in the last
moments of his life for a stabilizing identity that, for all his bravado, is
dependent on the approval of his two silent audiences: the "brethren"
at the column's base and the godhead above. Although this dramatic
monologue's two nonspeaking audiences seem barely present, it is
their influence (real or imagined) on St. Simeons's valuation of self
that makes the dramatic monologue the appropriate form for the kind

of psychic conflict this poem demonstrates. The dramatic monologue celebrates the speaker's subjectivity but at the same time denies his autonomy by assuring dependence on the validation of silent "others." That Simeon uses the pronoun *I* eighty times in this poem of 220 lines (or approximately once every three lines) attests to his egoism, but Simeon's subjective exhibitionism is at the same time a defense against the terrible fear of cosmic insignificance; the repeated *I*, a manic attempt to stabilize identity beyond the threats of isolation. This anxiety surfaces in Simeon's compulsive need for approbation; like all pilgrims, Simeon asks the question "What am I?" (124), but he depends more on his audiences for self-definition than traditional pilgrims do. Although Simeon may try to take on the role of chief actor by making himself the cynosure of all eyes and the director in telling the people how to behave in order to reach his blessed state, he is also acted upon as a puppet of his audiences' expectations, and of his God's parental and authoritative will. St. Simeon is what today psychologists would call a "field-dependent perceiver."[2] The speaker, who "scarce can recognise the fields" he knows (39), cannot rely on his own judgment for self-determination because his judgment is riven by alternating feelings of shame and superiority. Throughout the poem, Simeon, like the confused speaker of "Supposed Confessions of a Second-Rate Sensitive Mind" (1830), vacillates between faith and doubt and, correspondingly, between an ideal view of himself (e.g., a miracle-working, Christ-like Saint) and a hateful one (e.g., a shamefully filthy and doubt-ridden sinner). Unlike the speaker of the earlier poem, however, who confesses himself to God alone and does not hallucinate, Simeon projects his conflicts onto two silent audiences, who, because of the form of the dramatic monologue itself, become a mirror to Simeon's mental disturbance.

Michel Foucault has written that the ascetic is a prisoner "of a kind of mirror interrogation."[3] The dramatic monologue with its interior audiences and psychic repartee provides this kind of "mirror interrogation" for Simeon, who casts the image of a divided self. Overestimating his ego, Simeon calls himself "an example to mankind, / Which few can reach to" (185–86); underestimating his ego, he describes himself as being "From scalp to sole one slough and crust of sin" (2). Although this kind of imagery to describe sin is traditional, Simeon's neurotic vacillations are not. In nontraditional ways, the "argumentative internal colloquies"[4] (William James's term) that result from these vacillations are personified in various ways by the silent audiences. I am adapting William James's phrase to suggest that the dramatic monologue with its silent audiences allows for these "argumentative internal colloquies" and simultaneously for the psychodramatic element of auditory imagery, both paranoid and wish-fulfilling. When, for instance, Simeon's ego ideal is threatened by a paranoid recollection of the "evil ones" who "prate / Of penances" he could not "have gone through" (96–99), the pillar saint tries to reestablish a more favorable view of the self by presenting his case before what James would call an "ideal spectator,"[5] in this case, a merciful and fathering God, a glittering angel with a crown, or a populace grateful for miracles he has wrought for them. The psychic battle in Simeon's mind between images of despair and images of hope, voices of praise and voices of mockery, is thus projected onto the silent audiences, who represent Simeon's inability to stabilize his identity, an identity that he searches for "out there."

Furthermore, Tennyson has so effectively used the form of the dramatic monologue in "St. Simeon Stylites" that the self, spectators, and surroundings blur in interchangeable ways, making it difficult to determine whether Simeon is really "seeing" or hallucinating. Simeon himself attests to his problem in perception when he wonders whether he has really "borne as much as this— / Or else I dream" (91–92). In fact, everything Simeon says he sees and hears is made questionable by Tennyson, because Simeon is "half deaf" and "almost blind" (36, 38); perched sixty feet on a column above his mortal audience, he "scarce can hear the people hum / About the column's base" (37–38), as though their voices were part of an auditory hallucination. Thus, when Simeon "hears" the people "shout, 'Behold a saint!'" (151) he may just be imagining this, because his condition and the fact that the audience cannot speak for itself in the dramatic monologue allow for auditory as well as visual hallucinations. Simeon, therefore, can never really trust approbation from his audience, because that approval is not definitive,[6] unless he, but not his reader, imagines it to be.

The problem of whether St. Simeon is hallucinating becomes central in the climactic part of the poem where a vision or hallucination of an angel with a blessed crown appears and vanished before Simeon's eyes:

> Is that the angel there
> That holds a crown? Come, blessèd brother, come.
> I know thy glittering face. I waited long;
> My brows are ready. What! deny it now?
> Nay, draw, draw, draw nigh. So I clutch it. Christ!
> 'Tis gone: 'tis here again; the crown! the crown!
>
> (200–205)

Since it takes more than one person to verify a miracle and the two verifying audiences are silent, the form of the dramatic monologue itself makes Simeon's "miraculous" vision problematic. That the angel should be described as having a "glittering face" that is seen by Simeon in a "flash of light" (11. 202,200) supports the view that the image may be hallucinatory rather than visionary. Such a hallucination would be the product of wish-fulfillment, since the "blesséd brother" is coaxed by Simeon to confer a gift of potency: the crown is an *idée fixe* of heraldic power. Although the reader is dubious about the legitimacy of the vision, Simeon, after some doubt, interprets what he sees as proof that will support his ego-ideal: that he is "whole, and clean, and meet for Heaven" (210). But Tennyson fills these lines with enough ambiguity to discredit that proof. When Simeon, for instance, begs the angel to "draw, draw, draw" (204) nearer to him, Tennyson is punning on the word "draw," so that it means both to bring the crown closer and to draw it more clearly as an image, so that Simeon can see that it is a clear sign that he is saved. The second meaning of "draw" reduces the status of the vision considerably. Furthermore, even at the moment that Simeon seems to have received the crown that is promised in Revelation to saints—"So now 'tis fitted on and grows to me, / And from it melt the dews of Paradise" (206–7)—he still has doubts: "Ah! let me not be fooled, sweet saints" (209). Once again, Simeon cannot trust what he sees, and neither can the reader. The "dews of Paradise" which "melt" from the crown may be nothing more than feverish sweat—Simeon had earlier complained about being "wet/With drenching dews" (112–13)—and the whole "vision" may be the product of a delirium. Nevertheless, Simeon, because he wants to be saved so badly, interprets his vision of the crown to be one of salvation. In analogous ways, the narrator of *Maud* will interpret Maud's phantom voice as one leading him to heroic duty, and Rizpah will understand the "shaking of walls" to mean that her dead son Willy has returned to protect her. In Simeon's case, it is appropriate that the lines "'Tis gone: 'tis here again" (205) should recall the ghost scene in *Hamlet*, because like Hamlet, who has to determine whether his father's spirit is benign or malevolent, Simeon has to decide whether the angel with the glittering face is real or a delusion.[7] Much as Hamlet chooses to believe the ghost, in part to justify his hatred of Claudius, Simeon interprets the vision of the crown to be miraculous, because to interpret the sign in any other way would make a mockery and a madness out of the "pure" existence he has tried for so many years to live.

But to an informed Victorian audience, as well as to a modern one, Simeon's visionary experience would be suspect. Nineteenth-century psychiatrists, who believed that any form of excessive self-consciousness (like Simeon's) could lead to madness,[8] were beginning to discredit formerly regarded visionary experiences as hallucinatory, whether they had been experienced by psychiatric patients, by literary figures (like Hamlet), or by historical saints. These experiences, once thought to be the product of *Ate*, divine or demonic intervention, or black humours, were in the early nineteenth century primarily considered to be the result of nervous disorders, somatic disturbances ranging from irregular circulation of the blood to epilepsy.[9] In addition, nineteenth-century psychiatrists, because they were no longer bound or guided by religious doctrines, theorized about the correlation between religious enthusiasm and madness. The French psychiatrist, Philippe Pinel, for instance, describes in *A Treatise on Insanity* a kind of pathological fanaticism that could well describe Simeon's. Pinel writes of how such fanatics hallucinate devils constantly upon them (cf. 168–75) and invoke their guardian angels after having "discharged with great rigour, the duties of mortification, fasting, and prayer."[10] In addition, the Victorian psychiatrist George Man Burrows writes in 1828 that "Enthusiasm and insanity bear such close affinity that the shades are often too indistinct to define which is one and which the other." He adds that "excess of religious enthusiasm . . . usually and readily degenerates into fanaticism; . . . and permanent delirium too often closes the scene."[11] Tennyson, who had read Burrows as well as Pinel,[12] draws an equally thin line between religious enthusiasm and insanity in "St. Simeon Stylites." Since Tennyson himself retained faith throughout his life in visionary experience, while he was also a follower of contemporary psychiatric theory, the distinction between vision and hallucination in "St. Simeon Stylites" and between religious enthusiasm and insanity is a crucial one to our understanding of Tennyson and his art. Yet it is a distinction that has been largely ignored by critics as a result of viewing Simeon as a caricature of religious hypocrisy rather than as a case study in topical pathology.

To be sure, there is ample evidence in the poem to support a satiric view of the pillar saint. Simeon is least modest where he deems himself most humble, self-indulgent where he regards himself as self-denying, and blasphemous where he appears to be most suppliant. Since Simeon feels that "no one, even among the saints, / May match his pains with mine" (136–37), he unwittingly becomes a simoniac, bartering with God for salvation. He hopes that all his physical payments will receive heavenly interest through transfiguration as a reward for extreme suffering: the white robe, palm, and crown, promised in Revelation, will be his fair rate of exchange for a lifetime of misery and abstinence. Recalling William Hazlitt's description of religious hypocrites, Simeon's self-love is "heightened by the

fear of damnation" as he prays "very heartily for the forgiveness of a
'multitude of trespasses and sins.' "[13] And like T. S. Eliot's Thomas à
Becket in *Murder in the Cathedral*, Simeon is tempted by a hidden
knowledge that "Saint and Martyr rule from the tomb,"[14] earthly
mortification leading to eternal glorification. Indeed, Simeon does
want his name and deeds remembered among those of the blessed
saints who are "registered and calendared" (130) beyond the dust and
bones of mortal limitations.

But while these ironies are present and relatively easy to tally, they
present only one side of Tennyson's St. Simeon. I agree with James
Kincaid, who argues that "to view the poem as satiric twists it into a
petty attack on a target that is trivial and far too easy. It also over-
simplifies by responding to . . . the monstrous in St. Simeon and
ignoring . . . the painful doubt, and the voice of simple humanity."[15]
Stylistically, the delicate balance in the poem between language that
indicts Simeon and language that humanizes him reveals that while
Tennyson is critical of his pillar saint's excesses, he also pities Simeon
since the excesses are the products of the kinds of renunciation,
spiritual doubt, and sexual repression that led to mental disturbances
in his own age.

Critics who regard Tennyson's St. Simeon purely as a hypocrite,
religious grotesque, or demonic overreacher rely too heavily on the
opening and closing lines of the poem (the most satirical in tone) in
their interpretations. While it is true that Simeon reminds one of
Napoleon when he tries to usurp heavenly privilege by crowning
himself,[16] his diction is not consistently aggressive; he also beseeches,
confesses, and questions. When, for instance, Simeon cries out to his
Lord "And I had hoped that ere this period closed / Thou wouldst
have caught me up into thy rest" (17–18), the desire for communion
with God reinforces the impression of a dependent child wanting to
be "caught up" in the arms of a loving but distant parent. Furthermore, unlike Browning's insanely confident Johannes Argicola, who
believes that even if he drank "the mingled venoms" of all "hideous
sins" he would still have "God's warrant," which would "convert /
The draught to blossoming gladness fast,"[17] Tennyson's Simeon, at
the end of his life during a moment of spiritual crisis, is terrified like a
child in the dark (cf. *In Memoriam*, 54:17–20), because if his penances go unrecognized by God, then the whole purpose of his life will
have been meaningless. Harboring much more neurotic insecurity
than the egomaniacal Johannes Agricola, St. Simeon combines the
diction of aggressiveness with that of childlike submission.

At times, Simeon actually sounds more like Tennyson's imprisoned
Columbus than he does an ascetic fanatic or a Napoleonic over-

reacher. Both monologists largely receive identity from dependence on religious doctrines and cultural expectations. The fifty-year span between the writings of these two poems indicates Tennyson's persistent concern with this theme. Columbus, whose "chains" were thrown around him by an ungrateful Spain, sounds like Simeon when he assures himself and his silent visitor that though "Racked as I am with gout, and wrenched with pains" ("Columbus," 231), he is ready to "sail forth on one last voyage" in the "service of his Highness" because he still hopes he is written in the "Lamb's own Book of Life / To walk within the glory of the Lord" (87–88). Like Simeon's, Columbus's faith in God is hopeful rather than faithful; moreover, both speakers regard themselves as martyrs and justify their suffering with the possibility of eternal rewards, even though their anger and aggressive diction at times imply an impatience with the inscrutability of God's justice.

But unlike Tennyson's Columbus, who though distressed reacts to his confinement in prison with relative restraint, Simeon, a self-willed exile, is portrayed as a male hysteric. His anality is reflected in his view of his body as filthy and diseased; his drive for purification is, in addition, a defense against a threatening libido that he has fervently tried to repress through celibacy, mortification, and isolation. Simeon has alienated himself atop a pillar from the rest of mankind not so much because he wants to make a spectacle of himself, but either because he fears that the people will contaminate him through temptation or because he will contaminate them by direct contact, because he believes he is "From scalp to sole one slough and crust of sin" (2). Simeon says that he chose his pillar to be "more alone" with his God (84), but his ambivalence is reflected when he calls that retreat both a "pillar-punishment (59) and an "airy home" (214). Like his own split attitude toward the self, the pillar is both a hated and an idealized place, a case of the self and the surrounding becoming one.

Similarly, Simeon's attitude toward his body is neurotically ambivalent. Having "sifted" all his thought to find a way "More slowly-painful to subdue this home / Of sin, my flesh, which I despise and hate" (55–57), Simeon had virtually castrated himself at the "white convent" (61) when he wore around his loins the rope "that haled the buckets from the well, / Twisted as tight as I could knot the noose" (63–64). The incident with the rope is described in William Hone's *Every Day Book*, one of the sources Tennyson used to write this poem.[18] According to Hone, Simeon had tied the rope so tightly around his body that it took "three days to disengage the saint's clothing." As in Tennyson's poem, it was an ulcer eating through the skin (66) that had betrayed Simeon's masochistic "secret penance"

(67). In Simeon's mind, it is the body that betrays; it is the body that makes Simeon aware that he is not a brother angel with a "glittering face," but a fallen man "conceived and born in sin" (120). Simeon's dread of his fallen nature is implied by Tennyson ambiguously when Simeon blames his conception into sin on "their own doing" (121). Typologically, the pronoun *their* may refer to Simeon's Adamic parents and the carnal sin that was passed down from Eden; psychologically, however, it may also refer to Simeon's own parents from whose carnality he wants to divorce himself. Therefore, when Simeon refers to his flesh (which would include his parents) as this "home of sin," he is, perhaps, not using the traditional body/home analogy, but alluding to his parents' "home of sin" which he forsook for an "airy home" nearer to God. This could psychologically explain Simeon's later childlike dependence on a fathering God, a fleshless and holy surrogate figure to substitute for the worldly role models he rejected.

Simeon, however, still being flesh of his father's worldly flesh, has strong sexual desires that are sublimated by religious fervor but hardly vanquished. While Simeon hates his body enough to flagellate it "with scourges and with thorns" (177), he is at the same time obsessed with his "home of flesh." In this respect, he is like the Nietzschean character who trains his conscience until "it kisses as it bites."[19] To be sure, in Simeon's case, the ascetic has become sensualized. The celibate pillar saint actually takes masochistic pleasure in his "superhuman pangs," because it is the only way he can find to glorify the body while maintaining the illusion that he is glorifying the spirit. But because these feelings are subconscious and forbidden, they mask themselves in nightmares and pathogenically in hypochondria.

Some of these forbidden, repressed feelings materialize in disguised ways in Simeon's nightmare of whinnying horses, monstrous apes and whining pigs:

> On the coals I lay,
> A vessel full of sin: all hell beneath
> Made me boil over. Devils plucked my sleeve,
> Abaddon and Asmodeus caught at me.
> I smote them with the cross; they swarmed again.
> In bed like monstrous apes they crushed my chest
> They flapped my light out as I read; I saw
> Their faces grow between me and my book;
> With colt-like whinny and with hoggish whine
> They burst my prayer.
>
> (166–75)

An ambiguous interplay of typological and libidinal imagery is evident in this passage. Here the fifth-century pillar saint is using traditional religious imagery—e.g., coals, hell, a vessel, the cross, demons—to represent what he perceives to be a *psychomachia,* or moral battle, between himself, the holy man with the cross, and a swarm of evil demons. (Similar typological imagery can be seen in the paintings of St. Anthony and in plays ranging from medieval drama to *Dr. Faustus.*)

While Tennyson is utilizing traditional religious emblems in this passage, he would also have been aware of the psychological implications of this imagery, since the Victorians regarded horrible nightmares as symptomatic of mental illness. Tennyson's knowledge of this becomes most apparent in "Lucretius," a later poem, but it is also evident in "St. Simeon Stylites." Simeon's and Lucretius's nightmares serve as necessary outlets for repressed desires. Both poems, in addition, make use of beast imagery to represent states of madness:[20] Lucretius dreams of satyrs and rough beasts, much as Simeon dreams of apes, horses, and hogs. Furthermore, in both dramatic monologues, the dreams are reported to silent audiences in a way that resembles the manner in which a patient recollects a disturbing nightmare before a psychiatrist. And in both poems, the speakers' nightmares reveal a "twy-nature" ("Lucretius," 194) that both speakers want desperately to suppress, so that they can consider themselves or be regarded as culturally superior and beyond animality.

Tennyson underscores the futility of Simeon's attempt to transcend his animality—he does the same with respect to Lucretius—when he has Simeon say that he saw the demons' faces "grow between me and my book" (173). In this line, the book becomes for Simeon what Foucault calls the ascetic's "interrogating mirror." The dark, repressed, and forbidden side of Simeon's nature peers at him from this antibiblical "text" of the self. In addition, animal sounds disrupt Simeon's prayer, because subconsciously Simeon wants to stop praying so that he can express the animal voices that are a part of his complete nature, that of the body as well as of the soul. Tennyson implies this ironically when Simeon comes close to sounding like an animal as he drowns "the whoopings of the owl with sound / Of pious hymns and psalms" (32–33); like the animals, he also "whines" when he clamours," "mourns," and "sobs" (6). Using this kind of echo between human and animal voices, Tennyson suggests that Simeon's voice and the animals' are not antiphonal, but complementary: both are needed to make Simeon a whole man. But like Lucretius, who also does not accept his "twy-nature," Simeon courts madness by trying to make the impossible division between an angelic and animal self.

In addition to the nightmare Simeon has that reveals the sexual component of his spiritual conflict—"all hell beneath / Made me boil over" (167–68)—there is also the external symptomatic clue of hypochondria. Tennyson implies that his speaker is a hypochondriac when he has the speaker complain of "coughs, aches, stitches, ulcerous throes, and cramps" (13). Although the tone of this line is satirical, the symptoms recall those in Robert Whytt's eighteenth-century profile of hypochondria which includes some other symptoms Simeon appears to suffer from: "extraordinary sensations of cold and heat" (cf. 12, 16, 113), "failure of eyesight" (cf. 38), and "nightmares or incubi" (cf. 166–74).[21] Although Simeon's age and continued exposure to the elements have certainly contributed to these complaints, the reader is not told how long Simeon has suffered from them. The impassioned lament to God, however, suggests long-term duration, and Simeon's contemptuous attitude toward his body leads one to believe that these somatic complaints are a form of conversion hysteria, in which psychic repression results in physical symptoms.[22] The hypochondria neurotically defends Simeon from the narcissistic view of the self as a martyr, angel, or god that religious fervor can produce. Furthermore, it is a physical punishment against the kind of self-inflation that is intolerable to the self-abasing part of Simeon's ego; it is the "pillar-punishment" internalized so that the "airy home" can be experienced.

Thus far, we have considered Tennyson's St. Simeon Stylites as a psychologically complex figure. But the kind of psychic conflict that Simeon experiences because of libidinal frustration and a compensatory form of religious mania is not limited by Tennyson to the eccentricities of a historically distant pillar saint or to an obsolete form of renunciation. For the nature of St. Simeon's spiritual crisis and his dread of animality make him culturally topical rather than anachronistically aberrant. Moreover, his psychological complexity is an expression of Victorian anxieties.

The Victorian age, described by Carlyle as being "destitute of faith but terrified at scepticism," makes a fitting backdrop for St. Simeon, who is tortured by the silence of the gods and whose faith must be verbalized passionately and insistently to assuage the fear that God or his justice may not exist except in hallucinations or in "storms of prayer" (7). Since Tennyson uses Simeon to address not only a fifth-century audience, but also an invisible Victorian one, Simeon's impassioned claim to sainthood may also serve as a defense of that claim in an age in which "dissolvent literature" had historiographically and scientifically disputed the legitimacy of visionary experience, miracles, and saints.[23] Like Simeon, the Victorians also suffered as a result of these progressive theories from epistemological uncertainties that were exacerbated by the tenuous rather than secure relationship between man and the godhead.[24] When Simeon laughs in the poem, "Ha! ha! / They think that I am somewhat. What am I? / The silly people take me for a saint" (123–25), this outburst is a sign of epistemological confusion, for the laughter is not merely mocking, condescending, or hypocritical, and variations on the question "What am I?" can be found in most Victorian spiritual autobiographies. Simeon's laughter is the kind of dark, mad laughter that Hawthorne's characters—e.g., Arthur Dimmesdale and Ethan Brand—blurt out when faith and doubt in their mental universes become maddeningly ambiguous and interchangeable. Situated like Carlyle's Teufelsdröckh in a "centre of indifference," St. Simeon Stylites, as his tripartite name suggests, is in a kind of limbo. Positioned on a pillar (*stylos*) between heaven (Saint) and earth (Simeon), spirit and body, faith and doubt, meaning and void, the speaker rightly views himself as "Unfit for earth, unfit for heaven" (3). And unlike Hopkins's speaker in "Nondum," who can have faith that "Thou [God] art, and near," even when "No answering voice comes from the skies,"[25] Simeon has lesss cause for confidence since his "guiding light" may be hallucinatory. Although Simeon may believe at the closure of the poem that he has reached Carlyle's "Everlasting Yea" when he calls for a priest to deliver the "blessed sacrament" (215), Tennyson once again draws a thin line between religious enthusiasm and insantiy when he has the speaker say that it is the "warning of the Holy Ghost" (216) that enables him to prophesy when he will die. Although "warning" might imply a privileged communication between Simeon and the Holy Ghost, being "warned" might also result from a paranoid delusion, suggesting that Simeon does not trust completely in God's grace. He is as dubious about his faith as Romney is about the capacity for forgiveness in "Romney's Remorse": Simeon's "I trust / That I am whole, and clean, and meet for Heaven" (209–10) is as tentative as Romney's "O yes, I hope, or fancy that, perhaps, / Human forgiveness touches heaven" (151–52). This kind of tension in "St. Simeon Stylites" between faith and doubt makes the poem topical, reflecting a Victorian as well as a fifth-century crisis of faith.

Also topical is the way that St. Simeon Stylites reminds one not only of overzealous Catholics, but also of the early nineteenth-century Evangelicals, whose dread of a punitive judgment and of the putridity of the flesh is similar to Simeon's. As Ian Bradley writes in

The Call to Seriousness, the Evangelicals were, above all, "obsessed with the judgment which awaited them at death"; the "perpetual fear of being found wanting when the Judgment came led . . . into agonizing sessions of self-examination," often resulting in "an orgy of self-criticism."[26] Tennyson's poem, too, dramatizes Simeon's dread of being found unclean and sinful at the time of Judgment; Simeon also indulges in an orgy of self-criticism by flagellating himself into a state of arousal that he sublimates into religious zeal.

Bradley's book also examines how Victorian writers like Dickens, Charlotte Brontë, Trollope, and Samuel Butler satirized the excesses of these Evangelicals, who were worthy of scorn and no pity. Although St. Simeon Stylites is also satirized for his excesses, Tennyson's speaker differs from traditional British figures of religious satire, like Robert Burns's Willie in "Holy Willie's Prayer," because he is not only comical and culpable, but also isolated, vulnerable, childlike, deranged, and dying. He does not have the hawk-eyed wealth of Trollope's bishops, the confidence of Browning's mad clerics, the social position of Brontë's Mr. Brocklehurst, the parental power of Butler's George Pontifex and Dickens's Mr. Murdstone, or the sexual prowess ("wi' Meg" and "Leezies's lass") of Holy Willie. Instead, Tennyson's St. Simeon, at the same time that he is falsely pious, proud, and self-righteous, is also a man who has driven himself mad with doubts that all of his abstinence and all of his severe penances may go unnoticed, unblest, and unrewarded, leaving him an empty shell—scarred and without a pearl. Had Tennyson wanted merely, or even primarily, to make the pillar saint a subject of comedy or self-mockery, he could have turned St. Simeon into a kind of Bergsonian machine, as Mark Twain does in *A Connecticut Yankee in King Arthur's Court* when he was his protagonist, the "Boss," run a sewing machine with St. Simeon's otherwise wasted "bowing energy." But unlike Twain or his contemporary British satirists, Tennyson presents the reader of "St. Simeon Stylites" not with a monstrous social climber, a child-baiting parent, or a depersonalized saint machine, but with a man fallible, obsessive, and self-torturing. Had this poem been written by an author who still regarded the insane as sinful beasts worthy of ridicule and no pity, the purely scornful response might be appropriate. But it is not appropriate in a poem where Simeon, called "The watcher on the column till the end" (160), is portrayed as an archetypal and an apocalyptic man, a sentinel forever scanning the universe for meaning beyond blankness, vacancy, indifference, and silence.

While Tennyson's Simeon is a Victorian in his dread of animality and in his spiritual apprehensions, the poem is radical in the sense that it suggests how religious enthusiasm may stem from sexual frustration and how madness may result from a too vigilant repression of natural desires, whether in the fifth century A.D. or in the ninteenth century. Although this interpretation conflicts with the prevailing opinion that Tennyson advocated repression as a social necessity,[27] the poem conveys that Tennyson also saw the dangers inherent in immoderate repression. For St. Simeon's sexual dilemma in A.D. 459, in addition to his spiritual one, finds a counterpart in the more "civilized" forms of repression that were common in Victorian England. As Brian Harrison exposes in "Underneath the Victorians," Steven Marcus demonstrates in *The Other Victorians,* and Elaine and English Showalter document in "Victorian Women and Menstruation," anxieties and misunderstandings about such natural processes and disorders as syphilis, menstruation, nocturnal emissions, masturbation, deaths in childbirth, and frigidity filled many Victorian couples with sexual dread.[28] Largely as a result of such fears, repression became a watchword, a kind of social imperative, and indulgence in sexual activity, where procreation was not the goal, was considered a vice that could lead to madness. At the same time, however, psychiatrists within this Victorian "guilt" culture (I am adapting Malinowski's term) were beginning to perceive a link between socially repressed sexuality and madness. For instance, in *Cases of Insanity* (1831), Matthew Allen warns that continence as well as overindulgence is a frequent cause of insanity.[29] And Robert Carter, an influential physician and contemporary of Tennyson's, addressed the social consequences of repression when he wrote:

> . . . an emotion, which is strongly felt by great numbers of people, but whose natural manifestations are constantly repressed in compliance with the urges of society will be the one whose morbid effects are most frequently witnessed.[30]

This Victorian, paradoxical double view of sexuality and mental health finds its way into "St. Simeon Stylites." Considering abstinence a social imperative, Simeon, sounding like the popular Victorian social reformer William Action,[31] prescribes vigilance and admonishes his people to mortify the flesh "with scourges and with thorns; / Smite, shrink not, spare not" (176–78). But such vigilance and mortification of the body's normal drives produce a masochistic kind of pleasure both in Simeon and in any society that subscribes to them. As Foucault, focusing on Victorian society, argues in *The History of Sexuality,* a culture perpetuates "spirals of power and pleasure" of a masochistic kind when it voyeuristically monitors a source of potential pleasure that it simultaneously and obsessively resists or condemns.[32] Tennyson's intuitive awareness of this dynamic between desire and punishment is most apparent in the oread/satyr scene in "Lucretius" (203–7), but it is also present in this earlier poem. Simeon, as we have seen, takes masochistic pleasure in flagellating himself and in running off his list of hypochondriacal complaints; furthermore, he turns overrestrained desire into religious enthusiasm. Similarly, in Victorian England strictures on sexual expression are conterminous with the increase in pornography and prostitution in the cities as outlets for repression. Like the attempt of Simeon, who tries to embody his ego-ideal through abstinence, yet is described—"From scalp to sole one slough and crust of sin"—as if he were suffering from leprosy or syphilis, the attempt of Victorian society to establish a collective ego-ideal through repression backfires ironically when it brings to the cities what it had denied in the households. Although St. Simeon does not typify more rational Victorians, he shows how a character (or a citizen) can become victimized when a society encourages cultural values that are overly restrictive of desire.

Tennyson suggests in "St. Simeon Stylites," as he does in *Maud*, that it is social forces as well as individual volition that lead to irrational behavior. He implies this when he dramatizes Simeon as having the potential (misdirected though it is) of being a cultural leader. That Simeon is potentially a leader emerges through parallel symbolism when one compares "pillar" imagery in this poem with strikingly similar imagery in *In Memoriam*. In the latter (113:12), Tennyson describes his beloved Hallam, should he have lived to be installed in Parliament, as "A pillar steadfast in the storm." This phrase clearly alludes to Exodus 13:21, but what is surprising is that Simeon imagines himself in the same way. Earlier in the elegy, with imagery that recalls Simeon's attempts to grasp the heavenly crown, Tennyson writes that Hallam would have been a man

> Who makes by force his merit known
>   And lives to clutch the golden keys,
>   To mould a mighty state's decrees,
> And shape the whisper of the throne;
>
> And moving up from high to higher,
>   Becomes on Fortune's crowning slope
>   The pillar of a people's hope,
> The centre of a world's desire. : . .
>
> (64:9–16)

Although it is clear that Tennyson—at least consciously—is trying to portray Hallam as an ideal nobleman and civic politician, it may be an oversimplification to see the pillar saint as Hallam's antithesis. Simeon also tries by the force of his words to make "his merit known" to God and the people below; he, too, "lives to clutch the golden keys" of St. Peter; and on pillars of varying sizes, he has gradually moved up "from high to higher." At this height, Simeon has also become the "pillar of a people's hope," their prodigy of suffering, since his saintdom would bring blessings to the community and reinforce the Christian belief in the sanctification of suffering. While one might argue that Simeon's gropings are satanic whereas Hallam's projected aspirations are angelic, the major difference between these two figures, given the parallel imagery Tennyson uses, is primarily one of temperament. One sees in Simeon's misdirected energies and ambitions the potential of a cultural leader, whose enshrinement by his worshiping masses attests to the kinds of values he embodies and those toward which his culture aspires. Since history records that St. Simeon Stylites was followed "in oriental Christendom by a succession of pillar saints extending over many centuries,"[33] his cultural influence cannot be regarded as negligible. Representing a deeply rooted cultural need (as well as a personal one), he, like Hallam, is "The centre of a world's desire."

Taking this into account, one discovers that the last two lines of the poem—"Aid all this foolish people; let them take / Example, pattern: lead them to thy light"—are ironic in more ways than the obvious. Although Simeon uses these words as an allusion to the *imitatio Christi,* the lines mock Simeon because he can readily be considered the foolish person whose pattern of behavior and "example," self-defeating and barbarous, are ones that only a sadistic God might aid and a masochistic people follow. Yet, Simeon himself has been a victim of following patterns and examples that his culture has glorified: he emulates the tortured lives of Christ and the saints and models his own behavior on theirs (48–53) in part because he wants to exceed their glory as a paragon of suffering, but more importantly because his martyrdom of the self is influenced or inspired to a pathological extreme by the expectations and even the imagery (the magical "crown") of his Christian culture. This culture made suffering an object of worship and art; it made denial of the flesh a saintly aspiration.

The people who "hum / About the column's base" (37–38) worship Simeon as an *imitatio Christi:* it is through the spectacle of his suffering that they are vicariously cleansed and saved. Although Simeon also tries to manipulate these people, indeed believes he is leading them, it is the culture that has invested suffering and renunciation with the kind of magical power that attracts the childlike Simeon. Simeon has ironically become not only the victim of his own ego-ideal, but also the ritual scapegoat of his society's desire for evidence of God's presence and power, for the community is eagerly waiting for God to reap "a harvest" in them (146) through the ravaged body of their martyred saint.

This is the kind of cultural expectation that John Stuart Mill denounces in *On Liberty*. Mill argues that the ideals of Christian morality are "negative rather than positive; passive rather than active," "because Christianity's 'thou shalt nots' predominate over 'thou shalt,'" making an "idol of asceticism" that "inculcates submission to all authorities."[34] Similarly, Simeon's evangelical terror of being found wanting at the Day of Judgment "inculcates submission" to the authorities of his two audiences whose validation he seeks. His manipulation of these audiences is a defense against his fear (and, at the same time, desire) of being judged and dominated by them. This is one of the "negative" results of submitting to the restrictions of a "thou shalt not" world. Tennyson anticipates Mill's point and takes it several steps further by using the form of the dramatic monologue to show how thin a line there is between religious enthusiasm and insanity. He dramatizes in this poem how fanaticism, masochism, and madness may result from the entrapment of essential desires, especially in "guilt" cultures that sanctify renunciation and repression or derive models of social conduct from them.

Tennyson's "St. Simeon Stylites," therefore, is much more than just an attack on Catholic asceticism[35] or religious hypocrisy. It is a nineteenth-century portrait of Renunciation raging and weeping, obsessively and humanly, as its central figure sits, like a gargoyle desiring Grace, in the interspace between a "centre of indifference" and "an everlasting yea." Furthermore, the poem mirrors spiritual and sexual dilemmas in Victorian society, because like Simeon who neurotically views himself both as a diseased sinner and as the worthiest candidate for saintdom, Victorian England perceived itself both as a disease-ridden industrial center and, ethnocentrically and imperialistically, as the hub of culture, an "example" and "pattern" for all less civilized nations if they, like Simeon's "foolish people," were to see the light. Tennyson's St. Simeon, therefore, is not alone in his paradoxes: the poem serves not only as an "interrogating mirror" for a historically distant and irrational pillar saint, but for Victorian England as well.

3

Maud
Narcissus and the Quest for Familial Reintegration

Like St. Simeon Stylites, the speaker of *Maud* (1855), Tennyson's most famous poem about madness, courts insanity by reinvesting his libido narcissistically in an object of love and worship—Maud—toward whom he feels great ambivalence. The narrator's attitude toward Maud vacillates in the way that St. Simeon's feelings about the mercy of a fathering God does, because to varying degrees the love-objects from which the speakers unconsciously seek identity and validation are a projection both of an idealized and a feared self. In both cases, it is the neurotic tension between these two absolute and mutually exclusive views of the self that leads to derangement. Both men would like to see themselves as exemplars in their society, but the emergence of their darker natures obtrudes upon this ambition. Rather than taking on the burdens of their humanity and its dual nature, both speakers, almost invariably and self-deceptively, project onto others their own psychic confusions. Much in the way that St. Simeon projects his double view of himself as the worthiest saint and the worst sinner, respectively, onto God and demons, the protagonist imagines Maud to be prideful when it is he who is most proud, predatory when it is he who lusts for her, and accusatory when it is he who is feeling guilty. Maud, however, also serves an an objectification of the speaker's ego-ideal, for at times she is described as being divine and heroic—qualities that the narrator would like to possess. He tries to attain these qualities by attaching himself symbiotically to Maud. For if Maud is worthy of his worship, then the protagonist in wor-shiping her becomes blessed.

Maud also serves as an ordering principle in a universe in which the narrator feels alienated: Maud's garden of love is the protagonist's wished-for sanctuary. Furthermore, the speaker describes the protec-tive power of Maud's beauty as

> the one bright thing to save
> My yet young life in the wilds of Time,
> Perhaps from madness, perhaps from crime,
> Perhaps from a selfish grave.

$$(1:556\text{--}59)$$

Beatrice-like, Maud is thus cast as a protective force of *cosmos* (beauty and order) that the protagonist hopes will guard him from mental and social chaos. Yet the opposite is also true, for at times Maud haunts the speaker, especially in his dreams and after his duel with her brother. Indeed, the speaker's reactions to Maud are mutable, for she regulates and is regulated by the speaker's moods, his desires and fears, almost in the way that the moon regulates the tides. Like the lovely shell of the Breton strand (2:49–56), Maud is at times considered by the romantic speaker to be a work "divine"; when the narrator feels love for her or loved by her, he becomes like the adaptive shell that can withstand "the shock / Of cataract seas" (2:73–74), because if Maud's smile "were all that [he] dreamed, / Then the world were not so bitter / But a smile could make it sweet" (1:226–28). When the speaker loses or fears that he will lose Maud, the "forlorn" shell (2:61) becomes his reality, daylight becomes a "dull red ball" (2:205), and madness becomes his "tiny cell" (2:1; and cf. 3:2).

One discovers, however, in comparing *Maud* with "St. Simeon Stylites" that there are more points of divergence than meaningful parallels. Set, unlike the earlier "historical" dramatic monologue, in Victorian England and critical of Mammonism (as we shall see, in its variant disguises), Maud primarily differs from "St. Simeon Stylites" in its complex, free-associative style, which imitates the speaker's erratic states of mind, and in its pessimistic emphasis on the family and the associated fear of inherited madness. The poem is also daring in its use of a subterranean theme of incest, which critics have, in the main, left unattended, perhaps because Tennyson covered his tracks when he described the narrator's love for Maud as "a pure and holy love" that "elevates" the protagonist's whole nature.[1] Evidence in the poem indicates that this conservative description of the speaker's love for Maud is as suspect as Tennyson's remark that the speaker in joining the war effort at the end of the poem has given "himself to work for the good of mankind through the unselfishness born of a great passion."[2] In both instances, Tennyson's notes say far less about the character of the narrator and the nature of his madness than the poem does. The prose, in this case (as *always* in Tennyson), is far less liberated than the verse.

Tennyson's original plot outline for *Maud* emphasizes the role that a childhood trauma plays in the narrator's mental decline:

> Shortly after the decease of his father, the bereaved young man, by the death of his mother, is left quite alone in the world . . . the sad experiences of his youth have confirmed the bent of a mind constitutionally prone to depression and melancholy.[3]

This excerpt from the plot outline indicates that the speaker's feelings of isolation stem from the deaths of both parents. Moreover, his depression and melancholy are inherited, since he is "constitutionally prone" to them. The inheritance comes from the father, who was melancholy and sufficiently depressed to kill himself when a business venture failed. The narrator's terror of being predisposed to his father's mental illness is evident when he exclaims, "What! am I raging alone as my father raged in his mood? / Must *I* too creep to the hollow and dash myself down and die . . ?" (1:53–54).

For a Victorian audience, this fear of an inherited madness would be especially meaningful, because while the issue of hereditary insanity has a long history, the Victorians became particularly fascinated and preoccupied with this problem.[4] Tennyson himself, as we know from his recent biographers, dreaded that he had inherited the "black blood" of his fathers.[5] In an insightful recent discussion of the Victorian preoccupation with inheritance, Ann Colley demonstrates that Victorian scientists and writers "simultaneously held society and inheritance responsible for any sort of aberrational behavior,"[6] no longer attributing such irrational behavior to demons or other unworldly forces. Even before Henry Maudsley, influenced by Darwin, wrote what may be the definitive text on inherited madness, *The Pathology of Mind* (1856), in which lines from *Maud* are quoted,[7] Joseph Adams devoted an entire book, *The Hereditary Properties of Disease* (1814), to the subject. In addition, Robert Burton's *Anatomy of Melancholy*, which was a Victorian bestseller that Tennyson had in his library,[8] provided information on hereditary melancholy and on the "spleen" from which the narrator of *Maud* also suffers.[9] The issues of inheritance and social responsibility for madness make *Maud* not only topical, but also a problematic and especially provocative poem.

With *Maud*, one can take the issue of inherited madness beyond genetics. First, this "inheritance" in *Maud* is a literary as well as a scientific one. As critics have widely noted, thematic and verbal echoes of madness from revenge dramas, gothic novels, spasmodic poems, and the opera can be heard throughout the poem, as the narrator variously recalls Hamlet, Romeo, Heathcliff, and Werther among others.[10] Second, the idea of an *inherited* madness may also serve in *Maud* (and perhaps in Victorian society itself) a defensive function. That is, a fatalistic belief in hereditary aberrational behavior, as fearfully self-reflexive as it may seem, actually absolves the inheritor from guilt that might result from repressed rage toward the parent who passed down the predisposition. In *Maud*, such anger toward the suicidal father is redirected into obsessional love, revenge, and finally patriotism.

Partially as a result of the issue of inherited madness, the problem of projection in *Maud* is complex, for in this drama the protagonist's view of himself is not only influenced by Maud, his *anima*, but also regulated by feelings that he has for his deceased parents. Furthermore, since the narrator is cast in the poem as an only child, his feelings of depression and melancholy are "confirmed" when he is suddenly thrust into the new role of orphan. Psychic conflict is inherent in this transition, because in this new role, the speaker is both autonomous as an orphan and needy as an only child for approval and other emotional attachments. Because the narrator is prone to despair, his new role as an orphan creates ambivalence toward the self, an ambivalence that is also projected onto society and all other characters in his realm. For instance, the orphaned speaker's feelings of being both narcissistically self-contained and ontologically insecure are reflected in his dual attitude toward society: on the one hand, the speaker feels superior to the society that he rails against (1, sts. 6–13); on the other hand, he desires to be a functioning part of that society. This is evident from his need to join the war effort (and a new male family of soldiers) at the end of the poem.

The speaker's self-esteem is also affected to a psychologically disturbing degree by Maud's brother, onto whom the narrator projects repressed feelings of aggression and sexuality. A defensive use of projection is evident when the brother, who smells of "musk and of insolence" (1:234), has the power (or is invested with the power) to *gorgonize* the speaker "from head to foot / With a stony British stare" (1:464–65). Here Tennyson adapts the Perseus/Medusa myth by relating it to two men, suggesting in the speaker's unconscious sexual envy of the "musky" brother a homoerotic tension, which is resolved in the brother's death.

Stylistically, Tennyson dramatizes the narrator's need to project his psychic conflict by "having different phases of passion" in the un-named narrator "take the place of different characters" from whom he derives his unstable identity and vacillating self-worth.[11] Tennyson reveals how unstable the protagonist's identity is by, on the one hand, giving each of the dramatis personae a separate identity and, on the other hand, by having the narrator draw each of those characters into his orbit of consciousness, thereby limiting their autonomy as he classifies them with his own feelings and mood changes. This stylistic device adds to the suggestion of the protagonist's incipient schizophrenia, because as Christopher Ricks maintains:

> The point is not simply that the hero of *Maud* is the sort of person who . . . has splendidly various "successive phases of passion"; rather, that he is so near madness—and does indeed go mad—that it is possible, apt, and compelling for "successive phases of passion in one person [to] take the place of successive persons." The dislocation of the self in the hero can be turned—with creative appositeness—to something that is lamentably like the company of successive persons.[12]

This psychic conflict is further exacerbated because the narrator's own sense of self (like St. Simeon's) is neurotically dislocated. The speaker idealizes himself as a romantic lover, social reformer, noble warrior, and heroic son, but fears that he may be an inadequate lover, a social outcast, a coward, and a faithless son. As a result, the narrator finds it increasingly difficult to differentiate his own vacillating moods, or "phases of passion," from his attitudes toward other familial members (both from his own family and Maud's) who have helped to shape or shatter his self-esteem. Tennyson also intimates in *Maud* that the unnamed, orphaned narrator's identity is shaped by making all other characters part of his mental atmosphere, so that he can have a feeling of control (in a lifetime seemingly ruled by fate), as a willful child or an autobiographer would, of those characters who he feels have shaped his destiny. But unlike a traditional biographer who orders the experiences of his life chronologically both by objectively and subjectively examining causes and effects, the disturbed narrator involuntarily free-associates, alternating scenes produced by a self-torturing and self-aggrandizing imagination. For example, in one passage the speaker's despair is echoed in the "scream of a maddened beach dragged down by the wave" (1:99). Self-torturingly, such imagery recalls the narrator's mother's screams and his father's being dragged down to his death. But in the next stanza, contemplation over possibilities of loving Maud makes the narrator exult as he correspondingly sees "A million emeralds break from the ruby-budded lime" (1:102). Transference of effects such as these indicates that the narrator not only invests his "phases of passion" in other characters, but also in successive views of nature.

As in the case of St. Simeon Stylites, the protagonist's psychic conflict and narcissism are products both of an idealized and hated view of the self. As Karl Abraham states in *On Character and Libido Development*, this kind of neurosis "presents a picture in which there stand in immediate juxtaposition yet opposed to one another [as in a mirror] self-love and self-hatred, an overestimation of the ego and an underestimation of it—the manifestations, that is, of a positive and negative narcissism."[13] Tennyson had already demonstrated his intuitive awareness of this conflict in "St. Simeon Stylites," where the pillar saint's "positive narcissism" and "negative narcissism" are respectively revealed in his alternating view of himself as saint and sinner, and he will repeat the pattern in "Lucretius," where the enlightened philosopher wrestles with his own "twy-natured"ness (194). Furthermore, since Tennyson called *Maud* his "little *Hamlet*,"[14] it is worth noting that this kind of melancholic narcissism would have been readily accessible to Tennyson in most of Hamlet's soliloquies, some of which, incidentally, he imitates in *Maud* (e.g., 1:330). Hamlet, like the narrator of *Maud*, alternately overestimates and underestimates his ego. On the one hand, he regards himself as a man whom no one can (or dare) outwit; on the other hand, he curses himself for being "a rogue and peasant slave." Like the protagonist of *Maud*, Hamlet would like to think of himself as a loyal son and hero, but he dreads that he is faithless and a coward; furthermore, both protagonists redirect their anger from their parents to society, which is regarded as predatory, rank, and corrupt. In *Maud*, however, Tennyson stylistically represents the psychic split between his narrator's "positive and negative narcissism" by using antiphonal verse paragraphs. In these verse paragraphs, good moods of mind and brisk, easy thoughts alternate with bad moods of mind and gloomy, heavy thoughts.[15] We have already seen one example of how this works in the comparison between two emotional projections—the maddened beach and the bejeweled lime—and this pattern can be seen throughout the poem. This pattern imitates what Victorian psychiatrist Matthew Allen described as the alternating states "of excitement and depression" he found as symptomatic of insanity.[16] Furthermore, Tennyson's antiphonal verse paragraphs represent melancholy as a "contraction and dilation of spirits used of old to denote sorrowful and joyful moods, respectively."[17] Tennyson's style, therefore, imitates a pathology of mood changes in the narrator by alternating verse paragraphs of exaltation with those of despair.

But the operations of these alternating mood changes in *Maud* are not absolute or mechanical or always predictable, because the speaker is filled with ambivalence, especially toward Maud and his father. The narrator, trying to reintegrate the self that was damaged by the traumatizing deaths of both parents, seeks to reestablish his identity by reinvesting it in Maud. Although Maud is given a separate identity and dramatic history in the poem, the narrator, through whose focus the poem is shaped, can hardly regard her as existing except *for* him or *against* him. Maud is alternately perceived by the narrator as threatening—a predator looking for "fatter game on the moor" (1:74)—and as beatific—the sunlight breaks "from her lip" (1:275)—in her womanhood and in the kind of love she can offer him. The narrator's inability to reconcile these two qualities of womanhood is apparent, at first, in his desire to make Maud both transcendent (Beatrice-like: a flower, a voice, a star, a sunbeam, a queen) and eroticized (a temptress, a cheat, a *belle dame sans merci*). The speaker has obviously developed an unrealistic and romantic attitude toward love, which is demonstrated in the way he perceives Maud both as a goddess and a temptress—as if she, like many women in Victorian novels, could be nothing in between.

For a modern reader, however, Maud can be viewed as the speaker's *anima,* his ideal and feared self embodied in the guise of an omnipresent woman. The progagonist's attempts to make Maud transcendent and erotic are, thus, actually self-reflexive and narcissistic. This kind of narcissism is revealed when the narrator calls Maud "Life of my life" (1:657) and when he oddly admits both "if *I* be dear to some one else, / Then some one else may have much to fear" and "But if *I* be dear to some one else, / Then I should be to myself more dear" (1:529–32). The riddling use of "some one else" that is both dear to the self and feared suggests that the speaker is projecting his own narcissistic ambivalence onto Maud, who becomes the mirror for that ambivalence toward a feared and idealized self. Furthermore, the speaker's self-love and self-contempt are compounded by possessive and idolatrous feelings he has for Maud. The narrator, who believes that when Maud closes her door, "The gates of Heaven are closed" (the image is both spiritual and sexual), also maintains, like a possessive child, that his betrothal to Maud at birth "Sealed her mine from her first sweet breath. / Mine, mine by a right, from birth till death" (1:724–25). Although Tennyson is obviously borrowing Petrarchan imagery when Maud's door is compared to the "gates of heaven," the narrator's possessiveness of Maud is too ridden through with anxiety and guilt to be merely derivative.

Part of the narrator's guilt and subsequent ambivalence toward Maud is caused by his having fallen in love with the daughter of the man who he claims is responsible for his father's suicide and his mother's resultant depression and death. As Ronald Weiner contends, it is this ironic chain of events that sets into motion the speaker's neurotic vacillations between *eros* and *thanatos* in the poem.[18] Indeed, in this poem, love does "Spice his fair banquet with the dust of death" (1:654). From the opening lines of the poem, love and death are guiltily joined: Maud's "little wood," a place of love, is linked syntactically with the "dreadful hollow" (1:1), a place of death; the mythical Echo, the beloved of another Narcissus, can answer only " 'Death' " to whatever is asked her (1:4); Orion, the slain lover of Eos and Merope, lies portentously "low in his grave" (1:101). Later in the poem, the red roses of the speaker's passion for Maud are likened to blood (2:316). Therefore, the poem as well as the speaker's troubled mind becomes a landscape of love and death, and the speaker can never love with security because he is afraid the beloved one will abandon him, as his parents had done.

Still, the speaker's anxiety over Maud is more complicated than this. His idealization of Maud and of his own mother is, as Freud would maintain, "also a defensive process."[19] But from what or whom is the narrator defending himself? Throughout the poem, the narrator's hazy yet intense and coalescing recollections of his and Maud's families lead one to surmise that the speaker is struggling with some form of incest anxiety. Incest is a subterranean theme that runs through this poem (as it does in *Hamlet* and *Romeo and Juliet*, two plays to which *Maud* has been likened).[20] According to Weiner, the speaker is searching in Maud for a lost mother: "Maud is both the desired and forbidden love-object, and his emotional relationship to her is thus similar to the psychological dynamics of mother-love."[21] The blurring of Maud's identity with the mother's is evident when Maud's "passionate cry, / A cry for a brother's blood" (2:33–34), echoes the mother's "shrill-edged shriek" that divided "the shuddering night" (1:16) when the narrator's father died. Both screams will ring in the narrator's heart and mind like a requiem bell, "till I die, till I die," for Echo can paradoxically answer only " 'Death' " to whatever is asked her. The blurring of identities is also suggested in the empathy the narrator feels for Maud when he describes her mother, whose idealized love for Maud mirrors his own toward his mother. Perhaps, therefore, when the narrator says possessively that Maud is "Mine, mine by a right, from birth till death," he is not only addressing Maud, but also his own mother, whom he is unconsciously recalling, as a child might.

Although Weiner and most recent psychoanalytic critics focus almost exclusively on the speaker's mother as the primary source of the narrator's Oedipal anxiety and consequent problem with Maud, the father also plays an important part in the speaker's ambivalence toward himself and Maud. The narrator's ambivalence toward himself is at least in part a product of his mixed feelings toward his father.

Ambivalence toward the father as a suitable role model and provider is alluded to several times in the drama. Although the protagonist envisions his father as a victim—"Mangled, and flattened, and crushed" (1 : 7)—of a business venture that left him and his mother not only impoverished, "Vext with lawyers and harassed with debt" (1 : 705), but also emasculated—"flaccid and drained" (1 : 20)—part of the speaker's unresolved childhood trauma resides in repressed rage toward his father, who "had made false haste to the grave" (1 : 58). Children have little understanding of the causes and conditions of death: similarly, the narrator's recollection of his father's death is veiled in nightmarish imagery of shuffling steps and wailing winds (1 : 9–16). Consequently, after the death of a loved one, children generally experience mixed feelings of suppressed rage and subsequent guilt for that forbidden rage. At the same time that they are subconsciously angry at the parent for no longer gratifying their needs,[22] they blame themselves—"Villainy somewhere! whose?" (1 : 17)—for being somehow responsible for that death. Later in life, as in the narrator's case, if they still have not reconciled themselves to the loss of a loved one, perhaps because of unresolved guilt or anger, they may search for scapegoats to bear the unexpressed share of their guilt. The narrator does this when he searches society for villains and seems to find them everywhere (1, sts. 6–8). He projects aggressiveness, cowardliness, and cruelty onto others, like Maud's father, who is seen as the embodiment of evil. This is a safe (i.e., guiltless) way for the narrator to vent his spleen. But some of that anger is actually being directed away from its primary target, the father.

Weiner makes a strong, if speculative, case for the guilt's being Oedipal in origin. According to Weiner, the father died at a critical stage in the narrator's development when he (as a child) may have fantasized about possessing his mother by destroying his father. Consequently, when the father actually vanished from the home and died, the son felt responsible and guilty as a result.[23] There may, however, be other reasons for the narrator's ambivalence toward his father. The speaker's feelings of loss would have been intensified after his father's death because he was an only child and, therefore, was burdened with the sole responsibility of looking after his mother. As a result, he probably became even more emotionally attached to her: "For who was left to watch her but I? / Yet so did I let my freshness die" (1 : 693–94). He is also resentful that he had to sacrifice his "freshness," or youth and vitality, because his mother became overdependent on him in her depression. At a time when he needed nurturance to make up for the sudden loss of one parent, his mother regressed into her own private world of melancholy. This compelled him to nurture her without reciprocity. Thus, he was left painfully alone and helpless, to hear his "own sad name in corners cried" (1:261) and to watch his mother's "faded cheek / When it slowly grew so thin, / That I felt she was slowly dying" (1:702–4). "Villainy somewhere! whose?" Part of the blame must have been directed toward the absent father: "For who was left to watch her but I?" But such blame is redirected to society, because that is a less personal target; to Maud's father, who becomes the personification of evil; and to the self, because in blaming himself, the narrator can hold onto the image of his parents as the victims of society and of Maud's father. These are all ways of absolving guilt by transferring anger. Furthermore, because the speaker's father, his primary role model, committed suicide, the narrator is afraid he will do the same; he is left, as a result of his father's death, to question his abiltiy to survive in a world so filled with plunder: "And the whole little wood where I sit is a world of plunder and prey" (1:125). The speaker is also terrified (and guilty because he is) that he has inherited his father's physical as well as mental weaknesses. He alludes with defensive indirectness to his father's cowardice when he bewails, "And ah for the man to arise in me, / That the man I am may cease to be!" (1:396–97).

Ironically, even in the speaker's most pleasurable recollection of his father during his wine-toasting betrothal to the newborn Maud, the father could be said to represent the very kind of Victorian Mammonism the son detests. Maud is treated like a commodity when the birth is toasted with the lines:

> 'Well, if it prove a girl, my boy
> Will have plenty: so let it be.'
>
> (1:299–300)

Although bartering was not uncommon in Victorian England, and although these words, which the speaker remembers fondly as though they were part of a fairy tale, could be taken as a token of the father's genuine concern for his son's financial security, that concern becomes problematic when one adds to these lines the ambiguous description of the father dangling grapes above Maud's "sweet purse-mouth" (1:71). While such imagery may be pastorally innocent, a possible pun on the word *purse* to describe Maud's mouth reinforces the idea that Maud is a commodity and that the eager father is battening her with grapes, recalling the wine with which he toasted her betrothal. This is not the only negative association that wine has in the poem, for peace is said to be "slurring the days gone by" in the vineyards where "a company forges the wine" (1:33–36), Maud's brother's wildness is associated with "wine and horses and play" (1:757), and the narrator describes mankind, after he has dueled with Maud's brother, as "feeble vassals of wine and anger and lust" (2:43). Perhaps, therefore, when the speaker says that he fears "the new strong wine of love" (1:271), the obvious metaphor of love and wine both being intoxicating is subsumed by a wine that alludes to a Mammonite love rather than a sacramental one.

Maud is a poem that not only "offers a deeply pessimistic view of marriage,"[24] but also offers a darker view of the sanctified Victorian family. In fact, *Maud* presents, almost at every turn, a dark view of the family, from the mother who "kills her babe for a burial fee" (1:45) to Maud's mother, who somehow "came to be . . . allied" with so vile a husband (1:479). Furthermore, the cycle of family deaths and vendettas in *Maud* recalls mythic dramas like that of the House of Atreus. Tennyson gives *Maud* the classical plotting of such a drama to show how even the Victorian family, with all its propriety, duty, and gender coding, could be infected from within. But in *Maud*, Mammonism and war take the place of plagues in classical dramas, and inherited madness takes over the role of Fate. This darker view of the family is also extended to include nature and society at large: "the sparrow [is] speared by the shrike" (1:124), and *an extended family* of warriors in the end of the poem are ready to add their "deathful-grinning mouths" to fuel the flames of war. The protagonist's family, therefore, is a microcosm of the "inherited madness" within nature and society at large, much as the plague in *Oedipus Rex* is an outward sign of familial corruption.

Along Oedipal lines, the protagonist's ambivalence toward his father (and, by extension, to society and nature) may help to explain the unusual degree of hostility, fear, and sexual envy he directs at Maud's brother. Although the speaker's impotent father would appear to be the antithesis of Maud's virile brother—"That oiled and curled Assyrian Bull" (1:233)—the brother could be regarded psychologically as a projection of the "dreaded father" who, "curving a contumelious lip," can *gorgonize* the speaker "from head to foot" (1:463–65), as though he were threatening the narrator with castration in front of the woman (Maud/mother) that he and the brother love. This kind of gorgonizing occurs in a passage that alludes to the crossroads scene in *Oedipus Rex*. The protagonist meets with Maud's brother and his intimidating riding whip (1:461) while crossing his path, much as Oedipus meets his unknown father, Laius, and his punishing goad where three roads meet in Phocis. It is the narrator's pride and rage, like Oedipus's, that lead the speaker to challenge a dreaded father figure in the guise of Maud's brother. Jonas Spatz has extended the Oedipal analogy by contending that the poem is actually translating the theme of love and death into an Oedipal drama:

> Maud's brother has become the head of the household, and she [Maud] has become his "mistress." The narrator, in his position as a helpless tenant on the estate, assumes the role of the child. He dreams of murdering his master and competitor and then marrying his victim's "mate." When the hero kills Maud's brother, the Oedipal fantasy becomes a reality.[25]

Whether the protagonist is really "a helpless tenant on the estate" or actually a sibling rival is debatable, but, in either case, the killing of Maud's brother is wrought with Oedipal tension. The Oedipal blurring of the narrator's father and Maud's brother becomes psychologically most intense when the narrator, after he has wounded Maud's brother, looks down and is not sure whether it is he or his own father that he is seeing: "Was it he lay there with a fading eye?" (2:29).[26] The doubling of the "red-ribbed hollow" as a setting of death and Maud's scream as an echo of the narrator's mother's shriek adds to the Oedipal confusion of identities. It is such blurrings of identity, incestuous by implication, that lead the speaker "Through cells of madness, haunts of horror and fear" (3:2). The deaths of Maud and her brother (or, at the very least, their disappearance from the poem) symbolize the final separation of the speaker from his parents and their surrogates. This complete loss of family leads to an abject realization of total and intolerable alienation. Madness becomes the inexpressible expression for this insufferable loss, for as Edgar says in *King Lear*, "The worst is not / So long as we can say 'This is the worst'" (4.1.29–30).

In the mad scene that follows the duel and the loss of Maud, Tennyson changes the language of his speaker to reveal insanity through the speaker's "instant, abrupt and rapid transitions from subject to subject" and through his instantaneous "makings and breakings of thought circuits," two kinds of insane speech patterns that Henry Maudsley describes in *Body and Will*.[27] According to Tennyson's biographers, the kinds of madness that Tennyson describes in this scene are based on what he observed at the hydropathic establishment at Malvern and on his reading of Matthew Allen's *Classification of the Insane* (1831).[28] In the beginning of the scene, Tennyson dramatizes the speaker's madness by employing hallucinations, as well as "wild and whirling words." The speaker is hallucinating when he tells an invisible audience, "Tell him now: she is standing here at my head" (2:303), and he displays his guilt-ridden fears of death and decay with Lear-like references to maggots, pits, cracking bones, poison, wolves, and vermin. Furthermore, he projects his instability onto others by hearing everyone else "blabbing" but himself. The speaker's fear that everyone knows his darkest secrets is expressed in the lines

> For I never whispered a private affair
> Within the hearing of cat or mouse,
> No, not to myself in the closet alone,
> But I heard it shouted at once from the top of the house;
> Everything came to be known.
> Who told *him* we were there?
>
> (2:285–90)

This last passage alludes to Luke 12:2–3 but is secularized by the speaker almost to the point of blasphemy, since the narrator is adapting Jesus' words to the multitude and turning them into a paranoid query about how Maud's brother could have known about his tryst ("a private affair") with Maud in the garden. The italicized *him*, however, is ambiguous, because it can also refer to the speaker's spectral father or even to an overseeing God, since the allusion is biblical. In addition, the "new-made lord" and even Maud (who had earlier been called a "cheat") are suspect, because it is possible that either he or she told the brother about the tryst. Even if they did not, the speaker can no longer trust anyone, even himself, for everything he says even in his most private place (i.e., his mind) "is shouted at once from the top of the house," as if everything he said or did were worthy or terrible enough to merit the world's ear. In this, he shares with St. Simeon Stylites a double vision of himself as a cynosure of all eyes and a reprobate worthy of the censure of the world.

The speaker's duplicity during the mad scene is also apparent in his attempts to separate himself from the other madmen he describes even though they are behaving in a similar antisocial way. The other social misfits in the asylum—a lord, a statesman, and a physician (2:268–78)—rebel against the social pressures that led to their madness by enacting the kinds of psychological reversals that George Man Burrows describes in *Commentaries on the Causes, Forms, Symptoms, and Treatment . . . of Insanity* (1828). According to Burrows, in cases of insanity,

> . . . the natural disposition is sensibly altered, and, without apparent reason, the gay become sad, the serious merry, the taciturn talkative; . . . the prudent negligent, extravagant, and speculative. . . .[29]

In comparable ways, the madmen in *Maud* act in complete opposition to their expected public roles: the lord prays to himself; the statesman betrays party secrets; the physician blabs the "case of his patient" (2:270–75). Although the narrator seats himself in a position of superiority by observing these "sicker" men and listening to their "idiot gabble," he is one of them in needing to confess to the world his infatuation and tryst with Maud. In part, madness for the narrator is a psychotic defense mechanism against having to communicate with others, to share a collective humanity (he wants to feel unique), or to take part in life's dreary rituals of love and death, "hurrying, marrying, burying" (2:250), for which he has the tragic examples of his family and Maud's.

But madness and the sensation of being buried alive also serve a more important psychological function for the narrator: they are psychotic manifestations of his ambivalence toward his father, *whom he is identifying with and rejecting* at the same time. He does this through the process of madness itself. His imagined burial in the womb of the earth leads to a kind of rebirth by the beginning of the next section. It is the psychic tension between identification with and rejection of the father that surfaces in the scene through the speaker's verbal abreaction. Although the narrator had earlier revealed his shame in his father's unmanly suicide by using the word *creep* in the line "Must I too creep to the hollow and dash myself down and die" (1:54), identification with the father's desire to do this is implicit in the narrator's echoing couplet, "Always I long to creep / Into some still cavern deep" (2:235–36). This is what the narrator imagines he has done when he envisions himself as thrust into "a shallow grave" (2:244), which is another kind of "dreadful hollow." When the narrator imagines himself to be buried alive, he is also identifying with his father, who is actually the one "Dead, long dead, long dead!" (2:239–40). As the pressures of the world left the father "crushed and dinted into the ground" (1:7), so the son complains hysterically of a somatic disturbance: horses' hoofs that "Beat into my scalp and my brain" (2:246–48). It is as though the son can only exorcise his guilt not so much by begging forgiveness of the spectral Maud or by winning sympathy from a maternal surrogate as by propitiating his father for whom he had ambivalent feelings. He does this by ranting as his father used to do, by feeling responsible for the death of Maud, his mother substitute, and by imagining himself to be, like his father, "buried" in madness. Yet this is the process through which the speaker simultaneously rejects his father and the disposition inherited from him. Even in seeking vengeance for his father, the narrator is trying to prove himself more manly than his father by surviving the malevolence and madness of the world and finding a way to master them.

Whether such mastery is achieved at the end of the poem when the narrator joins the British forces in the Crimean War is debatable, because Tennyson's attitude toward war in this poem is ambiguous, and his narrator as a spokesman for truth, like St Simeon Stylites, is unreliable. On the one hand, committing himself after Maud's death to a socially approved and noble action may be the path to sanity for the protagonist. In joining the war, the speaker of *Maud* could finally belong to the ranks of men who, in his heroine's Bellona-like battle song, are "ready in heart and ready in hand" to "March with banner and bugle and fife / To the death, for their native land" (1 : 170–72). Although a modern reader might readily wince at such jingoism, for a Victorian like the protagonist, joining the war effort (with bugles and fifes of altruism leading the march) would be a sign of manliness, a vital sign for the narrator who is trying publicly to free himself of the fear that he is constitutionally a coward, like his father. Conversely, in imagining himself to be a brave warrior, the narrator is trying to take on the role that a "more manly" father would expect him to take, that of a soldier who could bring honor rather than opprobrium to his land and to his family's name.

The protagonist's attitude toward war is also Victorian in the way that it resembles the view expressed by Victorian psychiatrist Robert Mann and by Tennyson, himself in "The Charge of the Light Brigade," a poem that Tennyson published jointly with *Maud.* According to Mann,

> Sad as open and declared war is, it has in it those touches of moral grandeur which make its horrors tolerable in comparison with the more dreadful social, and domestic hostilities, which seethe continuously in the dense populations of overcrowded lands.[30]

Certainly, Mann's "dreadful social, and domestic hostilities" concurs with the protagonist's descriptions of Mammonism in the opening section of *Maud,* so that it is possible to consider the narrator's position on war a popular, contemporaneous one. In addition, the speaker's feeling toward war is similar to that expressed in "The Charge of the Light Brigade," the last lines of which praise the noble dead for dying for their country. Nevertheless, while these contemporaneous attitudes toward war would seem to support the view held by the protagonist of *Maud,* the problem of the narrator's madness makes Tennyson's position on war, at least in the context of *Maud,* much more slippery than it is either in "Locksley Hall" or in "The Charge of the Light Brigade," and the narrator's attitude toward war much less stable than Robert Mann's position.

Referring to the reliability of the narrator, Tennyson stated that the speaker even by the end of the poem "is not quite sane—a little shattered."[31] Furthermore, in an unpublished letter (6 December 1855) to Archer Gurney, Tennyson had written:

> Strictly speaking I do not see how from the poem I could be pronounced with certainty either peace man or war man. . . . How could you or anyone suppose that if I had to speak in my own person my own opinion of this war or war generally I should have spoken with so little moderation?[32]

The caginess of this letter, in addition to the problem of the speaker's sanity at the end of the poem, encourages such an interpretation as Roy Basler offers when he argues, against the prowar view, that the narrator in choosing to battle is merely substituting one form of "compulsion-neurosis"—idealization of war—for another—his obsession with Maud.[33] With this in mind, one could add that, like Lucretius who wants to "massacre" the Oread and satyr for having aroused him sexually, the protagonist in joining the war effort is primarily turning frustrated sexual love into a sublimated form of aggression: the red roses in Maud's garden of desire become the "blood-red blossom of war" (3:53).

Tennyson allows for such divergent interpretations by giving his speaker throughout the poem, but especially in the closure, rational as well as ironic lines to speak. The speaker's mood does seem to improve when, sounding like Ulysses, he says, "We have proved we have hearts in a cause, we are noble still" (3:55), or when he offers the platitude "It is better to fight for the good than to rail at the ill" (3:57). His self-perception also seems to have widened when he prognosticates, ' "It is time, O passionate heart and morbid eye, / That old hysterical mock-disease should die' " (3:32–33). But at the same time, Tennyson combines these words of reason with war imagery that is both ironic and infernal. For instance, while the speaker may boast of war's ability to make light "leap, / And shine in the sudden making of splendid names" (3:46–47), one recalls that the new-made lord's "gewgaw castle" is also said to "shine / New as his title, built last year" (1:347–48). If this parallel in imagery is intended to be ironic, then war, though highly esteemed by the narrator, can be regarded as another form of Mammonism that the speaker, purely as a result of self-interest, deems noble. The component of self-interest is also conveyed in the lines "Though many a light shall darken, and many shall weep / For those that are crushed in the clash of jarring claims, / Yet God's just wrath shall be wreaked on a giant liar" (3:43–45). Although the speaker is ostensibly alluding to Russia as "a giant liar" that "God's just wrath shall be wreaked on," the "giant liar" may also be a projection of Maud's father, since the image of being "crushed in the clash of jarring claims" recalls the speaker's father who was also "crushed, and dinted into the ground," because of a "jarring claim"—"a vast speculation" that had failed (1:9). If the "giant liar" also signifies Maud's father, then the protagonist, in joining the war forces, is imagining himself monomaniacally as the God whose "just wrath" shall be wreaked not only on his country's enemy, but also on his own.

Perhaps the most ambiguous image in the conclusion of *Maud* is the "blood-red blossom of war," which recalls not only the roses of passion in Maud's garden, but also other references to blood. Throughout the poem, blood is predominantly associated with evil, whether it be the hallucinatory "silent horror of blood" that drips from the "red-ribbed ledges" and on the "lips in the field above" (1:2–3), the mythical, revenging blood that is sprinkled by "the household Fury" (1:715), the prideful blood that is shed in a duel, or the hereditary blood from which the speaker believes he has inherited his disposition. Although the speaker at one point makes what would seem to be a pivotal distinction between "the red life spilt for a private blow" and that which is shed in "lawful" war (2:331–32), he is still in the asylum when he proclaims this and still believes he is buried alive; therefore, his utterance is not reliable. Furthermore, the red blossom is a variation on the roses to which Maud is repeatedly compared. But although one could interpret the "blood-red blossom" to be a distillation of Maud's passion that has been transmuted into the purifying blood of heroism, the narrator first compared Maud's roses to blood while he was in the asylum: "And I almost fear they are not roses, but blood" (2:316). This hysterical kind of transposition suggests that the protagonist's imaginings of blood are primarily pathological rather than sacramental—death's blossom united in blood with love's.

Is the speaker, then, suicidal or heroically inspired by love when he embraces "the purpose of God, and the doom assigned" (3:60) in going to battle? The verb "embrace" suggests that in the speaker's morbid fancy, love and death are embraced, for instead of embracing Maud or the memory of his parents' doom, he has now opted to embrace God's "assigned" doom. This kind of fatalism, however, is not new to the narrator: in a way he had already been "assigned" or fated to doom in having inherited morbidity as his disposition and a string of deaths as his destiny. Therefore, while the speaker's attitude may have changed, his circumstances are similar. Whether the narrator's destiny has actually changed by the end of the poem, however, remains ambiguous. Tennyson ensures this ambiguity in the conclusion by adversely blending the narrator's reasonable tone with ironic imagery and by having even the speaker doubting himself when he says that he has "awaked, as it seems, to the better mind."

Although these factors make the closure of *Maud* problematic, the narrator, in becoming a warrior, does seem to have certain needs gratified that were not fulfilled in his being either a son or lover. By joining the war forces and feeling that he has finally become "one with my kind" (3:59), the protagonist is attempting to escape the threats of isolation, lovelessness, incestual anxiety, and inherited madness that are associated with his family and its tragedy. To do this, the orphaned speaker substitutes a new, temporary family and system of patriarchal authority—a brotherhood of warriors overseen by virile Mars and his escutcheon (3:14)—for the nonviable one his morose and suicidal father bequeathed to him. Much as the speaker in worshiping Maud could feel blessed himself, now in joining a group of heroic warriors he can feel manly, virile, and significant. In joining this manly brotherhood, the narrator hopes that the man he was "may cease to be." But Tennyson leaves the reader to question whether the protagonist of *Maud* will ever be able to escape his inherited destiny.

The ambiguous closure of *Maud*, the themes of Mammonism and inherited madness, the vacillations between *eros* and *thanatos*, and the subterranean theme of incest in the poem all suggest that Tennyson was grappling in this poem with the relationship between the self and the "other" and with the influence of the family on madness. The tension between the self and "other" is most apparent in the protagonist's narcissism and in his symbiotic attachment to Maud. Such a Romantic attachment fails in a Victorian poem in which social duty (fighting for one's country) is favored above personal gratification. Yet, as we have seen, the speaker's decision to join the war effort is predicated on selfish motives: the extended family of warriors will provide a mirror to the speaker's manliness where he once saw only the reflection of his father's inability to survive the malevolence of the world. The dividing line between egotism and altruism in *Maud* is obscured because narcissism in the poem is the psychological equivalent of Mammonism: both are based on an economy of self-interest in which the grandeur of the "self" is dependent on the exploitation of some "other."

The influence of the family on madness is also central to *Maud*. Of

all the poems Tennyson wrote, *Maud* is the one he felt most personally about; he read it every chance he could, and could not tolerate
the poem being criticized.[34] Cristopher Ricks and other recent biographical critics have attributed Tennyson's fondness of *Maud* to the
wide range of personal experiences it dramatizes in various disguised
ways. Ricks regards *Maud* as an "audacious exorcism," an "intense
and precarious attempt" by Tennyson to "encompass," from the
security of a laureateship and a happy marriage, "the bitter experiences of four decades of a life in which many of the formative
influences were deformative."[35] Although this biographical assess-
ment by Ricks could lead one to believe erroneously that these four
premarital decades in Tennyson's life held nothing but bitter experiences, the critical consensus is that *Maud* is filled with biographical
substitutions for family members and friends. The germinal line of
the poem, "Oh! that 'twere possible," was written in grief over
Arthur Hallam's death; the "vast speculation that failed" alludes to
Tennyson's failed "pyroglyph" (wood carving) venture with his one-
time friend and business partner Dr. Matthew Allen; the protagonist's
raging father shares the disposition of Tennyson's own father; the
woman upon whom Maud is modeled, Rosa Baring, was also an
unrequited love interest for Tennyson because of the differences in
family fortunes. In each case, Tennyson was deeply hurt by the
people of whom he was fondest. But, conversely, each loss brought
an unexpected gain. For instance, Hallam's untimely death led to the
writing of *In Memoriam*, which brought Tennyson the laureateship;
Matthew Allen's insurance money allowed Tennyson to become inde-
pendent financially and artistically; Tennyson's father's early recogni-
tion of his son's talents shaped a poetic destiny; the rejection by Rosa
Baring and her family led to a happy marriage to Emily Sellwood.
Reflecting on these events and changes of fortune in his life, Tennyson
must have felt ambivalence toward these people from whom he both
lost and gained emotionally, financially, spiritually, and artistically. In
disguised ways, this ambivalence carries over into *Maud*, especially in
the speaker's mixed feelings toward his father and Maud. This is why,
finally, it is left to the reader's speculation whether tragic past experiences and inherited madness "assign" one for doom or motivate one
to victory. In *Maud*, neither Tennyson nor his narrator excludes from
probability the dual nature of destiny or the potential for human
growth that can be found or lost in madness.

4

"Lucretius"
The Fears That Throng the "Council-Hall"

> . . . the guilty conscience, terrified before aught can come to pass,
> applies the goad and scorches itself with whips. . . .
> —Lucretius, *De Rerum Natura*

In *Maud*, Tennyson had broken through a barrier by exploring how family, society, and individual predisposition contribute to madness. Using a contemporary character, he showed how psychic fragmentation and paranoia can result from narcissistic love attachments, and how ambivalence toward the love object may actually be a reflection of deep-seated ambivalence toward the self. Some of these conflicts— the narcissism, the psychic fragmentation, the paranoia, the alienation, the guilt—carry over into "Lucretius," but the form of "Lucretius" and its central conflict have more in common with "St. Simeon Stylites" than with *Maud*. Perhaps, it was the generally negative critical reception to the form and subject matter of *Maud* that fashioned this change. It is, however, just as likely that having broken through a barrier with *Maud*. Tennyson could now, through the safer distancing mechanisms of the dramatic monologue and a historical speaker, reinvestigate in "Lucretius," with less personal censorship, the problems of faith and the dynamics of dream psychology, sexual repression, and self-punishment that he had unveiled in "St. Simeon Stylites."

That noteworthy parallels exist between "Lucretius" and "St. Simeon Stylites" may at first be surprising, because one might expect, at least theoretically, Simeon's Catholic asceticism to be antithetical to Lucretius's Roman Epicureanism. Yet in both dramatic monologues, the historical title characters are scorned and pitied. Lucretius and St. Simeon ironically become victims of their seemingly secure beliefs and submerged desires. During the period of crisis that the monologues dramatize, each character, finding himself in an epistemological cul-de-sac, stares in horror and in madness at the void of his own meaninglessness, yet uses every defense at his disposal to avert his eyes from the abyss. In addition, displaying passive-aggressive personalities, these two men madly vacillate between feelings of cultural superiority and personal degradation.

Furthermore, Lucretius and St. Simeon—both speakers are Victorians in disguise—have tried fervently to repress their animality in an effort to become purer and worthier either spiritually or intellectually. St. Simeon has tried to do this by converting sexual energies into religious enthusiasm, while Lucretius displaces urgings of his libido with a form of "epistemophilia," or pleasure in gaining knowledge that is a derivative of sexual curiosity.[1] As a result of tensions produced by each form of sublimation, both speakers are haunted by nightmares, images from the libido that press "vast and filthy" hands ("Lucretius," 220) upon their will. Although the contents of these dreams are different—Tennyson had become more daring with psychological imagery after writing *Maud*—their psychological function is the same: they crack the mirror of self-idealization and compel the disturbed speakers to face the projected beasts that look in from the other side. When this happens, the conscience tries to reconstruct a center of tranquillity (in St. Simeon's case through faith; in Lucretius's case, through ratiocination) that the libido persistently demolishes with inner voices of doubt and desire.

Both poems also dramatize a Tennysonian and Victorian preoccupation with the tenuous, anxiety-producing relationship between man and the godhead. In this respect, Lucretius's plaintive address to the gods, "I thought I lived securely as yourselves" (210), recalls St. Simeon's lament to the deity, "And I had hoped that ere this period closed / Thou wouldst have caught me up into thy rest" (17–18). Although St. Simeon's need for a paternal authority figure in God is more childlike than Lucretius's, both speakers vacillate in their respect for such authority figures; they envy the power of the gods at the same time that they beseech them for stability and guidance, emotional as well as ontological. St. Simeon, who worships Christ, virtually challenges Jesus to "Show me the man hath suffered more than I" (1 48), while Lucretius, who admires Apollo, accuses him of being blind to his (Lucretius's) plight: "me . . . / . . . he sees not, nor at all can tell / Whether I mean this day to end myself" (144–46). In their ambivalence toward the gods, as well as in their fear of their animality, Tennyson's Lucretius and St. Simeon, though historically distant, are Victorians in their primary concerns and anxieties.

One critic, Charles Tennyson, who has noted the Victorianisms in "Lucretius," sees the poem primarily as a "protest against the materialistic basis of Epicureanism, with its denial of the immortality of the soul and of the existence of any divine guidance, and in its belief in the infallibility of the senses."[2] By juxtaposition, then, Victorian culture would represent, in its Christianity, the higher good, the saner belief, the truer light. While this kind of interpretation is plausible since Lucretius's philosophy mercilessly backfires as all attempts at ratiocination and transcendence fail, there is little in Epicureanism—and more in Christian Victorian society—to explain Lucretius's dread of animality or his desired attachment to the god-head, since sexuality is openly discussed in book 4 of *De rerum natura*[3] and the historical Lucretius was an atheist.

In Tennyson's poem, the speaker's dread of his animal nature far exceeds that expressed toward sexual desire by Lucretius in *De rerum natura*. In this classic work, which Tennyson read, Lucretius, though he warns man about becoming a slave of love, speaks without Victorian shame or censorship about such "forbidden" topics as sexual positions, masturbation, nocturnal emission, and the mutual sexual desire of men and women. While Tennyson's Lucretius is progressively more horrified by the sexual aggressiveness of women in the poem, and only idealizes Lucretia (a Victorian "angel in the house"), the historical Lucretius would not have been, since he felt that men and women were equally subject to desire: "Wherefore again and again I say, the pleasure is for both."[4] The extreme terror of sexuality in "Lucretius," therefore, is Tennyson's invention. In fact, the central energy of the work is not directed against Epicureanism but toward the problems of sexuality and identity confusion that confront Tennyson's maddened "Victorian" speaker. Moreover, the poem does not champion Victorian culture in counterpoint to the Lucretian world of "atom and void" (257); instead, "Lucretius," like "St. Simeon Stylites," poses a challenge to the moral benefit of constricting desire. And once again, Tennyson does this by focusing on the dynamics of madness.

The speaker's madness in "Lucretius" is informed by Tennyson's knowledge of nineteenth-century psychiatric theories on somatic derangement, periodic insanity, and lucid intervals. In the first twenty-five lines, or "frame" of the poem, Lucretius's self-loathing and consequent madness are attributed to a love philter, which his jealous wife, Lucilia, had procured from a witch and given him to drink in a misguided effort to "lead an errant passion home again" (17). Although the witch and the philter are the trappings of fairy tales, Lucretius's resultant insanity is not. The effect of the potion on the blood and on the brain (19–23) could well derive from Victorian psychiatric theories on circulation of the blood and consequential derangement. In *Commentaries on the Causes . . . of Insanity* (1828), for instance, George Man Burrows describes in somatic terms what happens when, as in Lucretius's case, "the chemic labour of the blood" becomes "confused" (20). According to Burrows, as a result of "accelerated circulation," "the imagination becomes more vivid, . . . and if the patient sinks into a momentary slumber frightful images present themselves and exhibit all the phenomena of delirium."[5] This is precisely what happens to Lucretius when he dreams of incubi after having drunk the potion. Burrows adds that when reason can no longer control the passions, because reason has been "disturbed or alienated," the "animal propensities which are implanted in all of us, will predominate."[6] Similarly, in Lucretius's case, the "brute brain" (21), or animal part, is aroused as the mind begins to lose its "power to shape" (23). Lucretius's kind of derangement is what Victorian psychiatrists would call "periodical or intermittent insanity,"[7] because throughout the poem the speaker is able to discourse logically on some subjects (e.g., the fall of the Roman commonwealth, lines 235–42) but reacts insanely to other images and ideas that have become obsessional (e.g., the hetairai and Helen's breasts). In addition, throughout the poem, Lucretius experiences "lucid intervals,"[8] or periods of clarity during which time he appears completely rational; but as the storm metaphor at the end of the frame portends, these momentary calms are repeatedly "mocked" by new emotional tempests (24–25).

While Lucretius's madness is informed by Tennyson's knowledge of early nineteenth-century theories on somatic derangement, it also anticipates by four decades Freudian theories on dreams, sexuality, and the inner workings of the subconscious. Had Lucretius been comfortable with his sexuality to begin with, an aphrodisiac would have had just the opposite effect that the love philter has on Lucretius: it would have made him ecstatic or at least comfortable in his lust; it would not have tormented him with images of a repressed libido. The content of Lucretius's three nightmares makes it apparent that the seeds of madness had been sown in Lucretius's subconscious long before the love philter had watered them. Therefore, the love philter primarily serves two seemingly opposite functions: it masks the sexualized component of the three nightmares by attributing it to external causation, and it reveals, like some dye injected into a vein, the inner workings of Lucretius's subconscious. In an analogous way, Lucretius tries to rationalize throughout the poem that the nightmare imagery is alien to his production of it, but is terrified at the same time that the only way to free his mind of the imagery is to kill himself, therefore making the self the source of menace.

Before Lucretius describes his first nightmare, he tries, as he does throughout the poem, to control his anxiety by displacing it. Lu-

cretius tries to circumvent responsibility for producing his first terrifying dream by appealing in a hypothesis to a collective and
philosophic *we*—"We do but recollect the dreams that come / Just ere
the waking" (35–36). Unlike St. Simeon, who overuses the subjective
pronoun *I* as a verbal defense against the nightmare of ontological
anonymity, Lucretius repeatedly uses the collective *we* not primarily
as a philosophical pose but, rather, as a way to escape the center of
feeling that the subjective *I* represents in its creation of libidinous
nightmare imagery. Therefore, frequently in the poem, and most
noticeably after each nightmare and hallucination, Lucretius seeks
security in the community of plural pronouns when he is terrified by
his own feelings. He imagines this "community" as a validating
audience; he does this as if he were trying to escape the narrowing
circles of his own desire by addressing or reaching out to a reading
public whose approval once made him feel superior as their
spokesman for truth. Lucretius also does this so that he will not have
to be alone with his visions, visions that progressively become more
frightening, proximate, and tangible as the poem develops in inten-
sity. But Lucretius's drive for a shared humanity (a collective *we*) fails
because he sees himself as set apart from other men; like Simeon, he
feels that he is closer to the gods than to man, even at the same time
that he hates his animal side enough to end his life when the gods do
not respond to his questions or offer any solace.

The sexual component of Lucretius's first dream, which anticipates
that of the next two, emerges when one looks at the kind of language
and imagery Lucretius uses in describing random creation and apocalyptic destruction:

> A void was made in Nature; all her bonds
> Cracked; and I saw the flaring atom-streams
> And torrents of her myriad universe,
> Ruining along the illimitable inane,
> Fly on to clash together again, and make
> Another and another frame of things. . . .
>
> (37–42)

While this imagery derives from *De rerum natura*, its nightmarish
quality does not.[9] At a cosmic level, the "flaring atom streams" that
"Fly on to clash together again, and make / Another and another
frame of things" (41–42) suggest sexual intercourse, both procreative
and destructive. The orgasmic nature of the imagery of flying and
clashing atoms is suggested by the words *flaring* and *streams*. Furthermore, since Nature is described as female ("her bonds," "her myriad

universe"), the "void" could represent the female other, which in each of the three dreams seems to threaten Lucretius to one degree or another.[10] According to Freud in *The Interpretation of Dreams*, "All dreams of the same night belong, in respect of their content, to the same whole. . . . [W]e must not overlook the possibility that these different and successive dreams mean the same thing, expressing the same impulses in different material."[11] In Lucretius's first dream, the words *torrents* and *Ruining*, both attributed to a female Nature, suggest the destructive quality of aggressive women, and this quality is carried over into Lucretius's other two dreams, respectively, of the hetairai and Helen. Furthermore, that the imagery of the first dream recalls the storm scene in *King Lear* may not be purely coincidental: Lear also invests in the brutal hurricane blasts the dreaded power and fury of his unfaithful daughters, who have lashed at him much as the torrents do. Yet, jointly with the imagery of destruction in this passage there is also that of procreation, implied by the lines "and make / Another and another frame of things." It would seem, then, that two kinds of "women" are displaced by this cosmic imagery: the genetrix and the destroyer. In "Lucretius," this duality also materializes in the two Venuses (85–102) and in the nightmare about Helen, whose breasts shoot flame (60–66). There also seems to be a connection with Lucilia, because like Nature who is described as cracking her "bonds," the undutiful and impetuous Lucilia defied her marriage bonds by giving her husband the love philter without his knowledge. As a result, just as Nature causes havoc ("Ruining") throughout the universe, Lucilia brings "havoc" to Lucretius's mind by giving him the sexually euphemistic "wicked broth" that *tickles* the "brute brain" (19–22). Consequently, the "juggernaut universe"[12] that Lucretius dreams about may also be a macrocosmic expression of the battle that is going on in Lucretius's mind as a result of Lucilia's being "mingled" with the "wicked broth." The reader can see how much Lucilia has, indeed, "mingled" with her husband's drink when Lucretius later hallucinates a wanton Oread, who imitates Lucilia's impulsive behavior—Lucretius had earlier rebuffed his wife's sexual advances (7–8)—when she is about to "fling herself / Shamless upon" him (202–3).

Appropriate to what is anticipated cryptically by the first dream and made more distinct and bold in the next two,[13] Lucretius posited in book 4 of *De rerum natura* that dreams could serve a wish-fulfilling function. Anticipating Freud's theory of dreams and wish-fulfillment, Lucretius writes of the kind of dream in which "one athirst often sits beside a stream or a pleasant spring, and all but swallows the whole river."[14] In the dreams that follow of the hetairai and the flaming breasts of Helen, Lucretius, the repressed pedant, approaches these streams of desire, but he is desirous of drinking from them as he is fearful of drowning in them. These next two dreams, though related to the first because of their sexual component, are more terrifying than the first because they represent the fear of interpersonal relationships and the dread of violation and sexual engulfment. It is perhaps for this reason that Lucretius tries to convince himself and his invisible audience that *only* his first dream was "mine, my dream, I knew it— / Of and belonging to me" (43–4), as though his other two nightmares were too terrible for him to claim ownership.

Lucretius's second dream, in particular, seems alien to his production of it. He imagines that all the blood shed by the Roman tyrant Sylla rains down on earth, but is baffled when "No dragon warriors [spring] from Cadmean teeth," which he thought his dream would show him (50–51). Instead, the blood-rain (and reign) gives rise to a threatening circle of hetairai, or prostitutes. Apparently Lucretius's bafflement results from something that would have been blocked from his consciousness of the dream had it not been for the catalyst of the love philter. The censored part of the dream may have something to do with Lucilia. Like the hetairai, Lucilia has been "curious in [her] art" (52); she has procured the philter from another curious artist—the witch (15)—and it is the drinking of the philter that unleashes the repressed "animalism" in Lucretius. Since Lucretius regards such animalism as vile, he projects that vileness onto the meancing hetairai rather than ascribing it to himself or to the bewitching Lucilia, who he does not know has given him a potion. In fact, throughout the poem, Lucretius, like Simeon Stylites and the hero of *Maud*, attributes brutishness and lasciviousness to others— e.g. Sylla, the satyr, the Oread, Venus, and Mars—instead of admitting the dark passions that lie within his own heart. Furthermore, in calling the Roman tyrant "Sylla" rather than by the more conventional Plutarchan name, "Sulla," Tennyson creates an echo between Sylla and Lucilia (as he later does with Lucretia and Lucretius). If Sylla is a pun on Lucilia, then "All the blood Sylla shed" could be an Eve-like allusion to Lucilia's menstrual blood, since Lucilia is also cast as a transgressor and a temptress. Perhaps this is why hetairai and not male dragon warriors spring unexpectedly from the rain of blood that dashes "the reddening meadow" (49). What terrifies Lucretius most in his second dream, however, is the way the hetairai surround him in "narrowing circles," as if to suffocate him (57). His terror of being touched by the hetairai reminds one of the touching phobia, or délire de toucher, of neurotics.[15] This fear is that being touched will annihilate volition and transform the person into the thing he hates, even when that thing is a projection of his own lust. The advancing hetairai tap the very source of Lucretius's shame in being "twy-natured" (194), or part man and part animal. Their "narrowing circles," like the interlocking Mexican dance in D. H. Lawrence's *The Plumed Serpent*, are part of a sexual ritual or initiation rite viewed by Lucretius, because he is sexually paranoid, as predatory, as if the hetairai were castrating maenads. Yet, it is his imagination that has conjured them, his desire that has produced them. Analogous to Lawrence's heroine, who faints as the male dancers circle in on her, Lucretius is torn between desiring the hetairai and being completely repelled by their embraces. This kind of conflict between a wish and a fear recalls Erasmus Darwin's theory (1796) that in "every species of madness there is a peculiar idea either of desire of aversion, which is perpetually excited in the mind with all its connections."[16] The hetairai become an *idée fixe* for Lucretius because they are the embodiments of his conflict between desire and aversion. Furthermore, Tennyson suggests that transference is occurring when he uses verbal echoes to confuse the identities of Lucretius and the hetairai. For instance, Tennyson has the speaker exclaim "Till I yelled again" (57) immediately after describing the hetairai also as yelling (56); the word *again* makes the identity of the one who yells in "Lucretius" as ambiguous as that of the one who shrieks (Maud or the protagonist's mother) in *Maud*. Tennyson blends their identities again when he has Lucretius tell how he "sprang up" (58) out of his nightmare much in the way that the hetairai "sprang" up from Sylla's rain of blood (49). Using these verbal echoes, Tennyson demonstrates the kinds of transference that can occur between the dreamer and his dream, especially when the dreamer dreads what he desires and desires what he dreads.

In Lucretius's third nightmare, the breasts of Helen materialize as the most striking and disturbing female image in the poem. Christopher Ricks attributes the allusion to Helen to Book 1 of *De rerum natura* in which Lucretius writes, "No love's fire fanned to flame because of Tyndaris, and glowing beneath the breast of Phrygian Alexander, would ever have set alight blazing battles of savage war."[17] Conversely, James Freeman cites Quintus of Smyrna's *The Fall of Troy*, adding that the dream is an "allegory which demonstrates how male power can be rendered impotent by female beauty."[18] While this interpretation is plausible, it is not "female beauty" that renders male power impotent in Lucretius's third dream, because it is not Helen, mythical or otherwise, but her "breasts" that are the source of the speaker's fascination and anxiety. This is verbally implied when Lucretius tensely repeats, "the breasts, / The breasts . . ."

(60–61), which compels the reader to regard them as an *idée fixe*. The third nightmare begins strangely with the phrases, "Then, then from utter gloom stood out the breasts, / The breasts of Helen." Lucretius reports this hesitatingly as though he were not sure at first whose breasts he was seeing. There is, in addition, a curious dislocation of chronology, appropriate in dreams but of significant consequence in this one. Lucretius's second dream supposedly ended at the "first beam of my latest day" (59), yet Helen's breasts stand out "from utter gloom." Although "utter gloom" may be an emotive state analogous to the darkness of the dreamer's mind (or the darkness of his mood) while dreaming, the juxtaposition of the phrases "first beam" and "utter gloom" imply an early traumatic memory. Since breasts are the fixed idea in this dream, the memory is one of infancy that is superimposed onto one of adult sexuality. The dream is Oedipal because the disembodied, phallic presence of a hovering sword, which challenges the female principle of Helen's breasts, sinks down impotently and "shamed" (63), because the woman's beauty reminds the invisible sword carrier (a projection of Lucretius himself) of an idealized figure whose nurturance he sought. The superimposition of an idealized mother figure onto the image of the seductive Helen (a glorified *hetaira*) makes the breasts an object of anxiety and cathexis. This anxiety is revealed symbolically when fire, instead of mother's milk, shoots out of Helen's breasts as Lucretius stares at them (64–66). Like the "flaring atom streams" of the first nightmare, this shooting fire represents the destructiveness of women that Lucretius fears. In this case, the idealized mother will no longer nurture her child because he has eroticized another woman; therefore, the flame shooting from Helen's breasts is Lucretius's punishment (like the fear of being smothered by the hetairai) for the sexual "crime" of voyeuristically longing for other women. The flame, thus, is both the speaker's displaced passion for Helen and his introjected mother's anger at her son for lusting after another woman.

Lucretius is sufficiently roused by this nightmare that he actually feels the flame and awakens at the unbearable moment of crisis. But his waking self has so censored the meaning of the dream from consciousness that all the speaker is left with is burning shame. In fact, he is disturbed by this dream to the point of contemplating suicide (103–4 and 146). Nevertheless, he tries to divert attention from his personal terrors by invoking Venus and Apollo, two powerful, surrogate parental figures, in search of pacifying cosmic explanations for his dream. Like St. Simeon Stylites, however, the passive-aggressive Lucretius beseeches these gods at the same time that he blasphemes against them, reminding "holy Venus" that it is his "rich proemion" that has made her famous (67–72), and accusing the sun-brilliant Apollo of being blind (145–46).

Lucretius's passive-aggressive behavior to the gods in general can best be seen in his treatment of Venus, which is a reflection of his similar ambivalence toward the women in his three dreams. Lucretius's invocation to Venus is a rhetorical tight-rope walk. First he insults her by saying that his lays will outlast her Deity; then he immediately apologizes, " 'Deity? nay, thy worshippers. My tongue / Trips, or I speak profanely . . .' " (73–74). Tennyson adds an extra dimension to this comic rhetorical device in dramatic monologues when he has Lucretius ask Venus coyly, almost teasingly, "Which of these / Angers thee most?" (74–75). But to avoid the sexual aggressiveness inherent in this question, the speaker reinvests Venus with power, making her the aloof one, by adding to his query, "or angers thee at all?" In fact, each time there is a danger of seeing Venus as an earthly woman, Lucretius turns her back into a goddess, or turns away from her. When Lucretius senses that he is transforming his own desire for Venus into his image of Venus subduing Mars (81–84), he suddenly recants to Venus, "Ay, but I meant not thee"—and then to an invisible, judging audience—"I meant not her" (85). Lucretius, who has beseeched Venus to seduce Mars to end the bloodshed in Rome, suddenly wants to dissociate himself from the libidinous Venus, who, like a glorified Helen, had ensnared Paris, Endymion, and Adonis, each love resulting in a form of destruction.

To resolve this conflict, Lucretius takes advantage of the fact that the Romans worshiped more than one Venus and shifts his attention from Venus Pandemos to the more maternal Venus of Cyprus, whose "all-generating powers and genial heat" (97) bring to mind a picture of a pastoral paradise, where "lambs are glad / Nosing the mother's udder, and the bird / Makes his heart voice amid the blaze of flowers" (99–101).[19] Several times in the poem, as in this instance, Lucretius imagines pastoral scenes of comfort for himself to avert anxiety produced by his darker thoughts. For Lucretius, the imagined pastoral scene is protective and regressive: the flames of passion, war, and punishment from the earlier nightmares become "genial"—a "blaze of flowers" takes the place of cosmic, flaring streams, and a threatening, unnurturing image of Helen's breasts is replaced by a "mother's udder" that is gently nosed by lambs. But unlike the bird, the lamb, or the flowers in this long-lost, golden world, Lucretius is plagued by a consciousness of mortality and a dread of animality that make his periodic and nostalgic returns to landscapes of innocence frustrating at best, self-torturing at worst. Perhaps this is the reason the speaker's mood changes so radically in the next verse paragraph, where Lucretius compares "the work of mighty Gods" with his own work and vacillates between a desire for suicide and a desire for immortality.

In this portion of the poem, Lucretius, like St. Simeon Stylites, envies the Gods their habitation and power at the same time that he admires them, because a comparison between himself and the gods makes him feel simultaneously both superior to other mortals and abjectly inferior to the divinities, who live in "sacred everlasting calm" (110), unaffected by Nature or human distress. The speaker, who harps obsessively on the "Gods" (five times in twenty-one lines) the way he had earlier been transfixed by storms and dreams (26–35), envies this "sacred everlasting calm," which no "sound of human suffering mounts to mar," because man may not gain such a calm even in dying (109–113). Unlike the speaker's pastoral reveries that are inevitably interrupted by reality, the God's pastoral habitation is eternal, and Lucretius is jealous of this. Sensing his inferiority to the Gods, Lucretius momentarily vents his hostility, like a willful child at an omnipotent parent, by using his philosophical intellect aggressively to dissolve the power with which he has invested the gods:

> The Gods, the Gods!
> If all be atoms, how then should the Gods
> Being atomic not be dissoluble. . . ?
>
> (113–15)

While this dissolvent speculation gratifies the aggressive part of Lucretius's nature, the thought is inimical to the passive side that still needs to feel there is a more powerful force in the universe than he. Like a child who suddenly becomes horrified when he realizes he has wished his parent-figure dead, Lucretius recants in a frenzy: "Meant? I meant? / I have forgotten what I meant: my mind / Stumbles, and all my faculties are lamed" (121–23).

Although one might argue that these lines satirize an Epicurean whose sophistical theories mercilessly backfire when the center of reason can no longer hold, the lines are also plaintive: the speaker is afraid he may be going insane. Having lost faith in the efficacy of his own intellect to solve the mysteries of life, Lucretius suddenly finds himself confronted with an uninterpretable world. The terror of this kind of world can lead a philosophical absolutist, like Lucretius, to madness. Furthermore, for Lucretius, intellectual chaos is related to sexual frenzy, because when intellectual certainty is no longer verifiable, where it was once the primary source of ego gratification, the libido takes over, and there is no way for long-lasting sublimation to occur, since the intellect, having lost its power to control feeling, can no longer make safe or viable substitutions. Lucretius, nevertheless, attempts to regain control by invoking Apollo, but this fails as did his earlier invocations to the gods, because he feels as ambivalent toward them as he does toward himself. In this instance, the speaker's ambivalence toward the sun god—his passive need to view him as all-seeing and his aggressive desire to perceive him as blind—shows that while Lucretius wants a superior force in the universe, he is at the same time envious of all powers vaster than his own. It is the speaker's unconscious envy, therefore, that makes the comfort of the gods inaccessible to him.

The support of the gods unattainable to him, Lucretius returns his attention to the world of man, but he returns to it in psychic turmoil. To reflect this turmoil, Tennyson uses a Miltonic epic simile that compares upheaval in the mind to political chaos in a "council-hall." The mental picture given is of crowds

> that in an hour
> Of civic tumult jam the doors, and bear
> The keepers down, and throng, their rags and they
> The basest, far into that council-hall
> Where sit the best and stateliest of the land?

(168–72)

Critics have generally focused on the political implications of this trope. Christopher Ricks, for instance, writes that Tennyson "is once again probably thinking of the French Revolution, one such event of which Carlyle compared to the Goths bursting into the Roman Senate."[20] And Henry Kozicki believes Tennyson is showing fear that the Second Reform Bill (1865) will lead to similar upheaval.[21] This kind of historical/political interpretation is valid, since it forms a link with two other historical reminders in the poem of "civic tumult": Sylla's tyranny and the "steaming slaughter-house of Rome" (47, 84) and the sundering of the Commonwealth (241). On the other hand, the allusion in these lines to Milton's description of "Satan and his Peers" entering the "spacious hall" of Pandemonium (*Paradise Lost*, 1:756–61) suggests that Tennyson may be adapting Milton's epic simile by turning his demonic invasion of evil into a psychological one. Given the psychological issues "Lucretius" raises, the epic simile may well be a macrocosmic representation of the breakdown of the mind, for later in the poem Lucretius describes how the Commonwealth is breaking "As I am breaking now!" (241–42). This parallel suggests that madness is caused by social forces or can, on a large scale, effect social chaos. In the epic simile, therefore, if the "council-hall," or seat of reason, may be viewed as the mind, the throng in rags, or "The basest," may represent the libidinous impulses that enter the council hall like lepers after they have overcome the "keepers," or defenses, that try to block access to the hall. The "best and stateliest of the land," among whom Lucretius (with his aristocratic knowledge) desires to belong, sit far into the council hall—away from the unsightly crowds outside the door. Since the "best and stateliest" (idealized selves or idealized community) belong to the earth and not to an impregnable outer world like the gods, the rag-throng is able to penetrate the fortress of the mind past all attempts of the conscience to keep the throng at bay. These leprous forces or libidinal ones, however, are part of the self or of the community; they become a riotous force when left repressed or unappeased. They would have less power or need to overthrow the "best and stateliest" of the land if their desires had been met or at least acknowledged as part of the mind's or the community's *twy-naturedness*. But when such forces are regarded as hostile "others" by the self or by society, their power festers as it grows.

Nevertheless, Lucretius believes, even though it is his imagination that has produced the rag-throng, that he is being physically abused by "others." He exclaims hysterically, " 'Can I not fling this horror off me again?' " (173) as if his own fears were physical manifestations beyond his power to control them. Like St. Simeon Stylites, who also tries to suppress his twy-naturedness, Lucretius is too threatened by his own libidinous impulses to realize that the "demons" that come between him and his idealized view of the self are products of the same consciousness, and not "others" sent to him by the gods as punishment for some unknown transgression. It is this kind of dissociation from the darker sides of their natures, bringing both Lucretius and Simeon to the point of madness, that waits for them, as well as society, at the very end of the "council-hall."

The threat of the rag-throng compels Lucretius to regress into another pastoral scene. This time he recalls the rustic myth of Picus and Faunus:

> 'But who was he, that in the garden snared
> Picus and Faunus, rustic Gods? a tale
> To laugh at—more to laugh at in myself—
>
> (181–83)

Although Lucretius laughs at himself for so childlike a fascination with a superstitious tale, the allusion to King Numa ("he") and the reference to laughter are significant. According to Ovid's *Fasti*, Tennyson's source for the myth,[22] King Numa snared the two pastoral lovers, Picus and Faunus, in a garden. The King shackled the two lovers and agreed to release them only if they would tell him how to avert the wrath of Jove and his thunderbolt. Although King Numa is gradually able to expiate his offense by joking with Jove, Lucretius finds "more to laugh at in myself" because only in tales is one able to pacify the gods' wrath, their storms and thunderbolts. In Lucretius's case, Faunus's admonition to Numa becomes destiny: "Thou askest great things, such as it is not lawful for thee to learn by our disclosure: divinities like ours have their appointed bounds."[23] It is these appointed bounds that Lucretius, of course, envies. The reference to laughter in this passage may also allude to Spenser's canto 6, of "Mutabilitie," in which Faunus is so aroused by his voyeuristic spying of the goddess Diana in her bath that "He could not him containe in silent rest" (st. 46)[24] and broke forth in laughter, which leads to his capture and punishment by Diana and her nymphs. Faunus's voyeurism in Spenser's tale and his punishment for a sexual crime find a parallel not only in the flames that shoot from Helen's breasts, but also in Lucretius's following hallucination of an Oread being chased by a satyr.

Lucretius hallucinates a pastoral scene in which, at will, "The mountain quickens into nymph and Faun" (187), as if his own imagination had become the "all-generating" power of nature (cf. 97). But unlike the first golden-age reveries, this pastoral scene, which is the product of a lustful wish-fulfillment fantasy, soon turns into a psychotic's punishing hallucination of voyeuristic panic and sexual guilt. And in this instance, Lucretius cannot distinguish between fantasy and reality because the two become interchangeable. This is primarily so because he has repressed his libido to the extent that he cannot imagine it or the unsurfaced desires it represents to be part of his waking identity. Yet he does not say, as he did before, that the images are from a dream. As the fantasy begins, an Oread appears, and Lucretius transfers his infatuation for her to a lusting sun, which "delights"

> To glance and shift about her slippery sides,
> And rosy knees and supple roundedness,
> And budded bosom-peaks—
>
> (188–91)

Although Lucretius has transferred his desire for the Oread to the sun, it is obvious that it is he who is eroticizing her by telescoping her "slippery sides" and describing her anatomy as "rosy," "supple," and "budded." But as the fantasy becomes fuller, a conflict develops between voyeuristic lust and puritanical repulsion. This conflict reaches a climax soon after a satyr—"Beastlier than any phantom of his kind" (196)—enters the pastoral landscape, similar to the way the rag-throng is imagined to enter the council hall. When the satyr lustfully begins to chase the Oread, Lucretius responds with volatile syntax and a string of plosive verbs that reflect his mental turmoil. As the satyr "draws / Nearer and nearer" both to the Oread and to Lucretius's subconscious realization that the satyr's lust is a projection of his own, Lucretius, in defense, volleys a spew of verbs at this darker side of his own nature: "I hate, abhor, spit, sicken at him" (199). His overreaction shows that he fears any kind of identification with the satyr; furthermore, to sustain the illusion that there is no similarity between them, Lucretius self-righteously assumes that the Oread, his anima, must loathe the satyr "as well" (200). He tries to will her into resisting the temptations of this evil one when he contains that very evil within himself. Imagining himself as the Oread's hero (if he rescues her, he also rescues himself), Lucretius casts himself as her nobleman—

> such a precipitate heel,
> Fledged as it were with Mercury's ankle-wing,
> Whirls her to me
>
> (200–202)

—so that he can convince himself that he is the moral opposite of the predatory satyr.

But Tennyson underscores Lucretius's sexual hypocrisy in the next few lines. Lucretius suddenly realizes that the Oread is not going to "whirl" her way toward him, but, instead, like a wanton, to "fling herself, / Shameless upon me" (202–3). That Lucretius should use the verb "fling" to describe the Oread's threatening advances is signifi-cant, because earlier he had cried out against his vision of the rioters, "Can I not fling this horror off me again?" (173) In both cases, Lucretius regards himself as the victim, even though the double function of the verb makes him both the passive receiver and the aggressive agent of flinging. He, however, only designates the "hor-ror" or "shame" as a force outside of his control, a force that torments him without provocation, like some ennobling tragic fate. The speaker's sexual hypocrisy becomes most apparent when he uses what David Shaw calls his "two-way syntax" in the next group of lines.[25] The ambiguous command, "Catch her, goat-foot" (203), refers both to the satyr and to Lucretius, since the satyr is catching up to the

Oread at the same time that Lucretius is about to catch the Oread in his arms. The same kind of transference occurs verbally in Lucretius's nightmare of the hetairai when both the hetairai and Lucretius yell in interchangeable ways. Lucretius, however, does not make the connection between the dreaded "others" and his own desires that Tennyson permits his reader to see and hear by using these kinds of word play.

As Lucretius distances himself from the Oread and satyr (both as a defense and a means to enjoy the chase voyeuristically), he invokes Nature with a sexually ambivalent, mixed command:

> Hide, hide them, million-myrtled wilderness,
> And cavern-shadowing laurels, hide! do I wish—
> What?—that the bush were leafless? or to whelm
> All of them in one massacre?

> (204–7)

At this juncture, the passive-aggressive speaker is so torn between sexual aversion and maddening lust that, like the "twy-natured" creature he had proved impossible (193), he splits, psychotically, both ways. He is shocked by an inner voice that suddenly rises to consciousness—"do I wish—What?"—and his extreme degree of guilt is conveyed by the fathomless image of a "million-myrtled wilderness," which recalls the "million horrible bellowing echoes" that break from the "red-ribbed hollow" in *Maud*. Lucretius is so aroused by the thought of seeing these "prodigies of myriad nakednesses" exposed, and simultaneously so repelled by his own arousal, that he converts sexual aggression into purging, warlike aggression, the way the tormented protagonist of *Maud* does when he joins the war effort. Lucretius ironically becomes like the tyrannical Sylla (or lusty Mars) in seeking to massacre "All of them." Because he is sexually paranoid, Lucretius imagines himself to be the persecuted when he is actually the persectuor. Yet to massacre these lovers is the conscience's way to hide Lucretius's lust from his own awareness (as it had done in his nightmares); at the same time, it is the libido's outlet for forbidden sexual desires and suicidal impulses in an act of self-purifying, socially sanctioned violence.

After once again invoking the Gods (207–12) for protection, security, and guidance, and not receiving them because he views the Gods as "careless" (i.e., without care, reckless, and unsympathetic), Lucretius tries to console himself with another pastoral scene. But this time the people and the landscape are experiential rather than mythical. Lucretius recalls lying on the grass with neighbors and discussing philosophy while partaking of "Only such cups as left us friendly warm" (214–16). Ricks traces the source of this pastoral scene both to *De rerum natura* (2:29–31) and to Horace's *Odes* (2.11.13–4).[26] But the imagery is also very similar in content and tone to section 89 of *In Memoriam*, in which the mourning speaker pacifies his grief momentarily by recalling how he and Hallam would discuss poetry and philosophy while sitting on the lawn and drinking from "the wine-flask lying couched in moss" (line 44). In these two instances, the pastoral reminiscence is a nostalgic attempt to recapture something now lost and once valued highly. In Lucretius's case, it is the "sober majesties / Of settled, sweet, Epicurean life" (217–18) that have been lost as a consequence of an unhappy married life. It is no coincidence that the love philter is the antithesis of "Only such cups as left us friendly warm" and that Lucretius's coldness to Lucilia in the beginning of the poem is in sharp contrast to the friendly warmth he had felt with his fellow philosophers. Although it is common, justly or unjustly, in literature to blame the philosopher's or the artist's loss of creative power on marriage (cf. Browning's "Andrea del Sarto" and Gissing's *New Grub Street*), the issue in "Lucretius" is not misogamy or misogyny, because the speaker's dread of animality is pathological; and Lucilia, like her love philter, is just a catalyst and not the isolated source of that dread. The next passage of the poem makes this quite apparent.

No sooner has Lucretius begun to reflect on a pastoral brotherhood than a hideous, punishing image of intellectual and physical violation invades his thoughts, the way the satyr had invaded the pastoral forest:

> But now it seems some unseen monster lays
> His vast and filthy hands upon my will,
> Wrenching it backward into his. . . .
>
> (219–21)

In insidious opposition to the remembrance of neighbors discussing philosophy warmly and freely on the lawn, this brutal and "unseen" monster defies the privilege of free thinking with a vengeance by manfully "wrenching" Lucretius's will "backward into his." Tennyson's use of the word *backward* is ambiguous since the word may not only have directional meaning, but also a Darwinian one since "Lucretius" and the *Origin of Species* are contemporaneous. Along with the earlier-used phrase "monkey-spite" (211), "backward" in the context of the poem may refer to the link between man and beast and the danger of retrogressing as a result of yielding to animal impulses.

Furthermore, before Victorian psychiatrists disproved the demonic causes of madness, it was held that the loss of will, one of the earliest and most prominent symptoms of derangement, resulted from "the work of some unclean spirit that has laid its hands upon the will."[27] Lucretius, thus, is once again laboring under the misconception that these darker forces are external to him when they are actually produced by his own punishing imagination. In addition, this waking nightmare is especially terrifying because it has suddenly come upon the speaker with a power and implied violence that are no longer distanced (or censored) by a pastoral setting. There are no "cavern-shadowing laurels" this time to hide the speaker from himself; furthermore, the abrupt switch in mood and imagery shows that Lucretius is losing track of the real world. His slackening ability to control his hallucinations is also implied by the physical proximity of the "unseen monster" to Lucretius, who is trapped in the embrace of "vast and filthy," molesting hands. Although the hetairai, satyr, and Oread threatened Lucretius's private space, they never touched the speaker, who has managed until this time to fend off such imagined embraces. But this beast is so much a part of Lucretius's strengthening libido, it is so powerful and mesmeric, that Lucretius no longer has the ability to resist it. Furthermore, for the first time, the central threatening force is described as male—"His vast and filthy hands." While the qualifers "vast" and "filthy" make the image so monstrous that it is hardly translatable, the sexual strength (implied by "Wrenching it backward") and contaminating animality of this unseen monster are apparent, since the imagery is suggestive of male rape. Yet, since Lucretius has also tortured himself with dreams and fantasies of overpowering women, this male variation on a theme appears to be more masochistic than homoerotic. Indeed, Lucretius seems to fall into the category of what Freud termed the "ideal masochist." To disguise the aggressive component of their sexual natures, ideal masochists—St. Simeon Stylites is another one—seek pleasure "in psychic chastisement." Freud adds that "such people may have counter-wish-dreams and disagreeable dreams," as both Lucretius and Simeon do, "yet these are for them nothing more than wish-fulfillments, which satisfy their masochistic inclinations."[28]

After his last hallucination, Lucretius, having found himself to be intolerably "beastlike" (231), is so disheartened that he begins to regard his whole life, except for his poetry which may immortalize him, as having been purposeless. Depleted verbally as well as physically of energy and the will to live, he describes how he is "Tired of so much within our little life, / Or of so little in our little life" (226–27). Lucretius's trancelike repetition of the word *little*—he utters the word four times in four lines, as if it were magical—may represent a regressive verbal attempt (pastoral scenes now having failed him) to defend himself from the "vastness" both of the "unseen" monster and of the vast unreasoning universe that threatens him with insignificance and oblivion. To make such fears less threatening and more manageable, he personifies life in a sentimental and unheroic way (cf. *Macbeth*) that displaces responsibility from the self: "Poor little life that toddles half an hour" (228). Then, Lucretius musters courage and changes his tone to that of a tragic hero: "Why should I, beastlike as I find myself, / Not manlike end myself?" (231–32). However, the bravura of this assertion is undercut when Lucretius compares himself not to a heroic warrior, but to a virtuous heroine—Lucretia— whose name he bears (235) and who was the victim of an actual rape:

> What Roman would be dragged in triumph thus?
> Not I; not he, who bears one name with her
> Whose death-blow struck the dateless doom of kings,
> When, brooking not the Tarquin in her veins,
> She made her blood in sight of Collatine
> And all his peers, flushing the guiltless air,
> Spout from the maiden fountain in her heart.
> And from it sprang the Commonwealth, which breaks
> As I am breaking now!
>
> (234–42)

Lucretia, the only historical woman in the poem Lucretius idealizes, killed herself after telling her husband, Tarquinius Collatinus, that she had been raped by Sextus, the son of Tarquinius Superbus. The legend deals with a sexual crime and its aftermath: as a result of Lucretia's suicide, the republic, or commonwealth, was established in 510 B.C.[29]

Although this historical information clarifies the allusion at a literal level, it does not explain why a number of words in this passage recall the beginning of the poem and anticipate the ending. For instance, it is curious that Lucretius should describe Lucretia as "brooking not the Tarquin in her veins" (237), when Lucilia had earlier been described by the narrator as having not "brooked" (14) her husband's lack of conjugal interest. To compound the confusion, both Lucretia and Lucretius make their blood, or commit suicide, in front of their respective spouses. Yet, Lucretia sheds her blood as the ultimate act of wifely duty, while Lucilia repents for not carrying out her duty, and Lucretius asks, "What is duty?" as if he had forgotten that marital duty includes sexual duty.

In one sense, this passage, with its verbal echoes and role reversals, represents a wished-for or idealized version of Lucretius's marriage. Lucretia, the antithesis of the sexually aggressive Lucilia, so embodies the Victorian ideal of a perfectly virtuous, self-sacrificing "angel in the house" that, like Mary Romney in "Romney's Remorse," she belongs in Ruskin's *Sesame and Lilies* along with other idealized, female role models for Victorian "ladies" to emulate. In addition, the commonwealth that "sprang" from the "maiden fountain" in Lucretia's heart recalls, antiphonally, the allusion to the hetairai that sprang up from Sylla's orgiastic blood rain/reign. Lucretia's blood that spouted sacramentally from her "maiden-fountain" to produce the commonwealth is also in opposition both to the flames that shoot from Helen's unnurturing breasts and the menstrual "reddening meadow" from which hetairai are spawned. This kind of interpretation would imply that Lucretia, like the "good" Venus of Cyprus, is the complete antithesis of all the aggressive, threatening, transgressing, and seductive women in the poem. Lucretius, therefore, could hold her in his memory as a sign that pure love and wifely solicitude are possible.

But this passage can also be interpreted as ironic. Tennyson may well be conveying a very different kind of message about the possibility of pure love in a world in which commonwealths can "break" (241), even though an act of supreme sacrifice led to their establishment. Since Lucretia is raped and Lucretius is violated by demons from his subconscious, it stands to reason that the reward for an idealized form of love in the real, unromantic, unmythical world is violation or madness or suicide. Lucretia's supreme act of love only forestalls chaos—the historical collapse of the commonwealth—and the effect of Lucretia's heroism on Lucretius's imagination is morbid rather than ennobling. Similarly, Lucretius's attempts to counteract erotic feelings with "Heliconian honey" (224) and other rhetorical placebos are failed efforts, because the "best and stateliest of the land" are still subject to the rag-throng, whether it enters the "council-hall" in the guise of a Tarquin or of some other satyr. The traditional Victorian strategy to suppress erotic feelings, therefore, is no solution, especially in such poems as "Lucretius" (and "St. Simeon Stylites" and *Maud*), in which pure or idealized forms of love lead not to good marriages, sanity, and salvation, but to unrequited relationships, warlike aggression, madness, suicide, or meaningless martyrdom. Lucretia's commonwealth breaks, as Lucretius's mind does, in a world where the pastoral garden coexists with the "steaming slaughter-house of Rome" (84). Finding "twy-naturedness" intolerable, Lucretius cannot reconcile these Apollonian and Dionysiac sides to the universe or to sexuality any more than Lucretia can. Both commit suicide when the world's pollution within their veins becomes unendurable.

Lucretius's identification with the chaste and heroic Lucretia also becomes ironic when one considers the way Lucretius kills himself and the language he uses as he is committing suicide. As he is about to end his life, Lucretius assumes the very role he and Lucretia had found abominable, that of sexual violator, and he finally localizes the soruce of menace within himself. While stabbing himself in the side like a depraved martyr, he rants:

> I woo thee roughly, for thou carest not
> How roughly men may woo thee so they win—
> Thus—thus: the soul flies out and dies in the air.
>
> (271–73)

The passive and aggressive sides of Lucretius merge in this act as he brutally stabs at a body that has been feminized in his imagination. Fittingly for the paranoid speaker, the language of sexual intercourse—"the soul flies out and dies in the air"—becomes the language of death.

Although the Romans considered suicide to be heroic, Lucretius's death in this poem is not heroic, nor are his futile attempts to repress his animality. The primary result of the speaker's suicide is his wife's frantic display of repentance. Beating her breasts, tearing her hair, and wailing her lamentation, Lucilia virtually manages to upstage her dying husband. Tennyson implies the egoism behind her grief when he writes that she "cried out upon herself" (276), like one of Dickens's hypocritical mourners in *Great Expectations*. In fact, the closure of the poem, rather than being an attempt by Tennyson to show a woman's proper remorse, reads like a parody of melodramatic scenes in Victorian novels:

> With that he drove the knife into his side:
> She heard the raging, heard him fall; ran in,
> Beat breast, tore hair, cried out upon herself
> As having failed in duty to him, shrieked
> That she but meant to win him back, fell on him,
> Clasped, kissed him, wailed: he answered,
>   'Care not thou!
> Thy duty? What is duty? Fare thee well!'
>
> (274–80)

The opening phrase, "With that," signals the artificiality of this passage. Although the frantic verbs—"ran," "beat," "tore," "cried," "shrieked," "fell"—used to activate Lucilia's grief suggest a sincere outpouring of emotion, Lucilia is treated by the omniscient narrator as though she were a machine pacing back and forth with hands upraised. Furthermore, for all of her classical grief and dramatic posturing, Lucilia is still petulant, falling on her husband as the Oread had threatened to do. Lucilia is left nameless in this passage; she is just a collection of actions, and those actions begin only *after* she has heard her raging husband fall to the ground.

"Raging" is a key word in this passage, and the difference between Lucretius's mad raging and his wife's socially approved grief (at least by Roman standards) is important. The closure focuses on socially approved grief rather than on mad rage, much as the opening lines of the poem had attributed Lucretius's crisis to the agency of a magical love philter rather than to preexistent causes of derangement (e.g., melancholia, mania, or prior somatic disturbance). The fairy-tale beginning and melodramatic ending of this dramatic monologue are so different in tone and tension from Lucretius's verbalizations and anxieties throughout the poem that it almost seems as though the two parts were written for different audiences. Furthermore, the joining of the two parts, frame and inset, may provide a subtle commentary on these two audiences. The closure of the poem would appeal to polite society that prefers a melodramatic or fairy-tale treatment of madness, as well as of love and desire. The narrator of the closure offers the finale as if he were a director at a stage rehearsal; like Lucilia, he stands behind the door (or frame) until Lucretius's raging has ended. The address to "duty" (which is more a Victorian than an Epicurean concern) prompts one to juxtapose the Victorian world with that of Lucretius. Although one might be tempted to take the conventional view that a poet like Tennyson would provide grounds for such a comparison to show the superiority of a "dutiful" society like the Victorian in contrast to a faithless Lucretian universe, the poem's central energy is in the opposite direction.

The Lucretius Tennyson has cast in this poem, much more terrified of sexuality and envious of the gods than the historical one, is a Victorian in sensibility more than he is an Epicurean. Since Lucretius is a puritanical yet subconsciously aggressive individual, his psychic conflict, resulting in suicide, is caused not by failing to repress sexual drives, as Ann C. Colley believes,[30] but by repressing them to the point that madness develops when a stimulant of love is introduced into his veins. Counter to the traditional Victorian view that repression of such drives is part of individual, marital, and social "duty," Lucretius questions that duty first with maddening nightmares and waking fantasies, and then with suicide. Lucretius's failure to surmount or placate the demons generated by his own denied libido demonstrates the failed attempt of puritanical man or society to enforce the repression of normal drives without undesirable and sometimes deadly consequences. Tennyson's "Lucretius" shows how repression does not prevent so much as encourage the rag-throng into the civic chambers of society or the mind. In a world where the "twy-naturedness" of a Lucretia and Sylla must, by necessity of good and evil, coexist, denial of darker and lighter tendencies within the self can lead, as in Lucretius's case, to needlessly assumed guilt, self-deception, displaced aggression, isolation, self-hatred, and suicide. In Victorian society pornography, prostitution, flogging, and imperialism grew, like Lucretius's nightmares, from the underside of an over dutiful, passive-aggressive culture that tried to see itself, at least in its polite novels and ethnocentric policies, as the "best and stateliest of the land." With this poem, Tennyson illustrates that passivity, propriety, politeness, duty, self-discipline, renunciation, and virtue may have a counterpart in evil that, when unrecognized by those too proud or hypocritical to see, may lead to madness or even death.

5

"Rizpah"

Mother of Sorrows or Mother Devourer?

Although Tennyson's most sustained and controversial treatments of madness in poetry center on male experience, the poet's interest in women's mental disturbances, their manifestations and determinants, is equally long-lasting. Early poems like "Mariana," "Fatima," "Oenone," "The Lady of Shalott," and later works like "Lancelot and Elaine" attest to the durability of this interest. In all of these poems, however, Tennyson links a woman's melancholia, mania, or idolatry to her consuming and frustrated passion (whether spiritual or sexual) for a male object of love, attachment, or power. We see this happening once again in "Rizpah" (1880), but in this poem Tennyson adds the important and intriguing elements of social injustice to a woman's lament and maternal nurturance to her obsessive despair.

A despair so deep that it leads to madness in a mother whose son has been publicly executed is the subject of Tennyson's poignant dramatic monologue "Rizpah" (1880). The nature of the mother's love, however, the primary source of her hysteria, and the social implications of her pathology are left open to interpretation. One of the most accessible paths to interpreting this poem, because of the pathological excesses of Rizpah's mourning, is the Freudian, but critics have left this path untraveled in their effort to idealize Rizpah's maternal love and devotion to her son Willy and to implicate the madder society that executed him for a petty crime—robbing the mail (21).[1] Comparisons with other Tennysonian poems on madness, and tensions within "Rizpah" (between sympathy and judgment and between mystical vision and hallucination), suggest an alternative, more subversive meaning to the poem. Although this meaning is concealed by the speaker's being named after a glorified biblical figure and by Victorian conventions—the beloved, dead child, the grief-stricken Madonna, the innocent victim, and the black-hearted lawyers—that frame the scenario, evidence in the poem reveals that Rizpah, as the embodiment of mother love, inhabits in her obsessional mourning the limbo between "Election and Reprobation" (73). Like Romney's Mary, she is in a poem in which "pure light" does *not* "live on the canvas" ("Romney's Remorse," 10). This darker meaning surfaces when one applies Freudian theories, especially those propounded in *Mourning and Melancholia,* to interpretation. Freudian theory counters traditional Christian readings of "Rizpah" by exposing the narcissistic component of the speaker's excessive mourning and smothering maternity. Using psychoanalytic theory in this way, one can free Tennyson's poem from the kind of sentimentality that has kept "Rizpah" from being read as a poem rich in psychological complexity.

According to Jerome Hamilton Buckley, Rizpah, "As the title should suggest, . . . is less an individual than a type, and the passion with which she defies all constraining circumstances is simply a quintessential mother love."[2] He adds that "Rizpah" "is in effect not a character study of great psychological complexity." Basing Rizpah's "quintessential mother love" on the suggestion of a title, however, is problematic, because although Tennyson derived the title "Rizpah" from a magazine that described the "sorry plight" of a "Brighton Rizpah,"[3] he originally entitled the poem "Bones."[4] If one can base interpretations purely on titles, Tennyson's original title for the poem may shed some light on Rizpah's fetishistic obsession with her son's bones. Certainly such an obsession—Rizpah not only collected and hid Willy's bones, but also, like a mad archeologist, "numbered" them (10)—makes one question the judgment that "Rizpah" is not a psychologically complex poem. Since the madness of Rizpah is Tennyson's invention—neither the "Brighton" Rizpah nor the biblical one was described as insane[5]—the nature of that madness needs to be considered seriously. To regard Rizpah merely as a "type" lacking psychological complexity is to reduce madness in the poem to a dramatic occasion when it is much more substantive. Interpreting "Rizpah" in this way not only simplifies the psychologically complex issue of mourning in the poem, but also minimizes Tennyson's ability to explore the peculiar dynamics of mother love, a kind of love that Tennyson represents in "Rizpah" as being both procreative and destructive.

The double nature of Rizpah as both creator and destroyer has not been discussed by critics, one suspects, because of the tendency, as a result of the religious imagery in the poem, to view Rizpah as a *mater dolorosa* in the likeness of the Madonna and to view the society she inhabits as a crucifying one. Joshua Adler, for instance, sanctifies Rizpah's maternity by likening her son Willy's execution on the "cursèd tree" (59) to the Crucifixion and the black-heartedness of the lawyers to that of the Scribes and the Pharisees.[6] Rizpah, thus, in her archetypal mourning takes on the role of the *mater dolorosa*, and her voice of sorrows becomes a criticism of society. Adler beleives, furthermore, that madness in the poem has an "ironic function," but that irony is directed solely at society and not at the speaker, because she and her son Willy are the innocent victims of social evils.[7] James Kincaid poses a comparable view that the evils of social judgments must be "cast aside" "in oder to live with the elemental love and devotion of Rizpah."[8] There is evidence in the poem to support both Adler's and Kincaid's conclusions. For instance, Rizpah's terrifying recollection of being seized, shut up, and beaten in a madhouse, because she "couldn't but hear that cry of my boy that was dead" (45–48), is as damning an indictment of eighteenth-century treatment of the insane—the poem is set in the eighteenth century—as one can find in Victorian poetry.[9] But there is also another side, a darker side, to Rizpah's maternity that is implied in her fixation on her dead son's bones, which she groveled and groped for (8) in the "loud black nights" (6). Rizpah's obsession with these bones, like St. Simeon Stylites' fixation on the crown, is not all sweetness and light. In Rizpah's case, a bestial groveling after a son's bones suggests a grotesque, rather than sacred, maternity, a devouring, cannibalistic kind of love, instead of a sanctified spiritual one. In *Mourning and Melancholia,* Freud describes a similar kind of narcissistic melancholia in which the "ego wants to incorporate the object into itself, and, in accordance with the oral or cannibalistic phase of libidinal development . . . it wants to do so by devouring it."[10] Furthermore, as in *Maud, eros* and *thanatos* are so intermingled in this poem—partially a function of mourning itself—that Rizpah, rather than solely being a *mater dolorosa,* takes on the guise of the mythical Great Mother, who is creator and destroyer both: "the creator and nourisher of all life and its grave."[11] It is the obsessiveness of Rizpah's mourning, resulting in auditory hallucinations (1–4, 45–48, 73, 82–86) and paranoia (5, 13–14, 59, 69), that reveals the double nature of her maternal love for Willy. Rizpah's persistent vigil and her idealization of her dead son are defense mechanisms against ambivalent feelings she has had for him. The *idée fixe* of her son's bones becomes the outward sign, pathologically, of this ambivalence; the bones convey the image of a mother both protecting the memory of a beloved son and devouring that memory, through introjection, so that her own sense of identity and purposefulness as a mother will not be negated by her son's untimely death. Similarly, the mythical Great Mother is not only the nurturer of life, but also the devouring mother that "draws the life of the individual back into herself,"[12] back into the womb/grave of her being.

In part, Rizpah's ambivalence toward her son is a product of mourning itself.[13] As we have seen in *Maud*, the loss of a love object produces a conflict between despair and rage that is normally resolved, though not in Rizpah's case, through the process of mourning. Rizpah's repressed rage at her son for abandoning her, bringing her family a shameful name (35), and causing her, indirectly, to be institutionalized, is at war with her idealized image of her son as a baby (20 and 53–54) and as a martyr (11. 34–37, 57, 59). Furthermore, when the loss is of a child, grief becomes exacerbated by the mother's feeling a "total sense of powerlessness" in not being able to protect the child she gave birth to.[14] Rizpah's intense desire to protect her son, ostensibly from predatory lawyers but more importantly from the actuality of death itself, surfaces when she tells her lady visitor, "I have gathered my baby together" (20) by collecting his bones, as if Willy were still umbilically tied to her by way of the magical bones. The curious thing about Rizpah's word choice is that it shows that she is as symbiotically dependent on Willy as he once was as an infant on her. Rizpah's acute separation anxiety from her son (usually it is the other way around) indicates that her sense of identity, ontological as well as physical, is threatened by her son's dissolution. Although it is common for a grieving parent to idealize a dead child and imagine seeing and hearing him in the early stages of mourning, Rizpah has been doing this for years. To bear the loss of her son, Rizpah imagines the elements charged not with a Hopkinsian "grandeur of God," but with the despair of Willy, a despair that takes on cosmic force as it infuses the entire world with wailing. It is as if not thinking of or hearing Willy's voice even for a moment will make his death final, real, unbearable. But in protecting Willy, Rizpah is also protecting herself, because her identity is fused with her son's. This is apparent when Rizpah, blocking out the adult image of her son, tries to introject the infant Willy by hysterically remembering the bones that "had moved in my side," "the bones that had sucked me, the bones that had laughed and had cried" (53–54). The image of bones in a womb is one of birth and death (an appropriate emblem for the Great Mother), and shows Rizpah's attempt to deny death by transforming it into an image of birth.

According to Freudian theory, in the process of mourning

the forsaken person transiently loses his self-esteem and affirmation of life, because the protest against the loss mobilizes unconscious hatred and resentment toward the departed love-object. Since the bereaved person is still dependent on the love-object, even idealizes the image of the departed, he has to turn whatever hatred and resentment there is against himself. This self-hatred threatens the integration of the ego as long as the protest rages against the loss. . . . The re-integration of the ego, and the return of self-confidence, depends on the acceptance of the loss.[15]

In Rizpah's case, loss of self-esteem and affirmation of life are not "transient," because the acceptance of the loss has not occurred and, thus, the reintegration of the ego has not been established. This is partially because Rizpah, like the protagonist of *Maud*, has redirected to society her unexpressed rage toward her son. Analogous to the protagonist's diatribes against Mammonism in *Maud* are Rizpah's invectives against black-hearted lawyers. Yet in rejecting society, Rizpah has no one to mourn with. Mourning is a social ritual, a ceremony, but Rizpah practices her own secret ceremony—collecting bones—in the night. She officiates at her own private ritual, and her sanity is the sacrifice. But better for her to do this than to admit her forbidden feelings of anger for her dead son. That anger, nevertheless, surfaces in Rizpah's mad words and acts.

Although Rizpah, when idealized like her son, may seem like a modern Antigone when she buries her son's bones against the dicates of society, or like Boccaccio's and Keats's Isabella when she kisses her son's remains (55), Rizpah's synecdochic fixation on bones belies the sentimentality of her actions. Her *idée fixe* of bones is as conflict-ridden as the protagonist's descriptions of his father's mangled body are in *Maud*. While one might argue that the bones become sacred relics in "Rizpah," in light of the Christian imagery and because bones were all the mother had left of her son, they can also be seen as fetishistic and necrophiliac, recalling the mad narrator's obsession with Berenice's teeth in Poe's story.[16] As a fetish, the bones become a magical weapon against the dissolution of death, homeopathically, even as they are a constant reminder of death.

Rizpah's ambivalent feelings for her son materialize in the different ways in which she perceives Willy when she is speaking freely (i.e., madly) and when she is trying to respond in ways she thinks are appropriate (i.e., rational, courteous ways) to her auditor, the lady in the room who has come to hear her deathbed confession (15). This charity worker serves several functions in the dramatic monologue. She serves the narrative function of getting Rizpah to recall her son's execution and to defend him; she also serves as a foil to Rizpah: she is childless and made only "for the day" (19), while the bereaved Rizpah is a creature of the night. But most significantly, the charity worker provides Tennyson with a method to reveal Rizpah's psychological complexity by showing how Rizpah regards Willy when he is the center of her attention or when the lady is her audience. Since Rizpah, more often than not, tries to temper her language when she is speaking to the charity worker (e.g., 11, 15, 81), it is appropriate that she should describe her son as a "good" mother would. In these descriptions, Willy takes on the traditional ("sane") images of a cuddly infant and a sporting youth, while Rizpah's role becomes that of the good wife (21) and protective mother. It is when that lady's pithy compassion and talk of sin and repentance (60–68) make Rizpah defensive and threaten her control over her emotions that the *idée fixe* of bones looms as a reminder of her derangement. The intermittent "discussion" between Rizpah and the charity worker would represent the "incubation" of her madness.[17] When Rizpah begins to talk without interruption, the associations she makes between love and death indicate that this "incubation" engenders madness. Also, when Rizpah does not realize the woman is in the room or when the woman's voice cannot be heard over her son's (82), then Willy's voice in the wind becomes that of a suitor—irresistible and dangerous—and not that of an infant or traditional Victorian son.

In the beginning of the poem, Willy's voice wailing in the night wind beckons Rizpah to come out while "the downs are as bright as day" (4), which would be a dangerous thing to do, because Rizpah believes the whole world, even the moon (4), is spying on them. Willy's words, therefore, are a kind of *dare* to Rizpah, much as Willy had been dared by his friends to rob the mail (29). The ambiguous line that follows—"We should be seen, my dear; they would spy us out of town" (5)—bespeaks an assignation, romantic interlude, or tryst, and not a familial meeting between a mother and child. Clearly there is role confusion in Rizpah's relationship with her son, which is symptomatic of her insanity.

In a way, Rizpah's predicament—whether to remain in her shelter or face her son's beckonings in the loud dark night—resembles that of the Lady of Shalott, who also has an inner voice. A "whisper" has told the Lady of Shalott that a curse will befall her if she looks away from her her mirror. She risks that curse when love for Lancelot fills her room. In an analogous way, Rizpah feels compelled to risk the safety of her shelter by heeding her son's luring voice. Because Rizpah has introjected her son and his voice, Willy becomes a kind of mirror in which Rizpah can either see herself as whole (alive because Willy still needs her to protect him) or part (dissolute because her function as a human being ended with her son's death). In both "The Lady of Shalott" and "Rizpah," love and death are intermingled because of a narcissistic yearning of the self for the other. In both poems, it is love and the search for new identity that lures the sheltered figure out of her sanctuary; and in each case, this love comes with the threat of death. But, paradoxically, each woman comes closest to expressing the truest, deepest passions of the self by intermingling love and death; the Lady of Shalott writes her name about the prow before she dies, and Rizpah feels the walls shake (85) in an ecstasy of passion mixed with danger.

From the above, one can infer that Rizpah's obsessive relationship with her son is more narcissistic than sanctified; her possessiveness of his bones, and, in her hysteria, his possessiveness of her whole being suggest a love darker and deeper than that of a conventional *mater dolorosa* for her martyred son. Since a husband is alluded to in the poem—Rizpah calls herself an "old dying wife" (21)—it is curious that so little attention should be paid to his absence (or death), and so much attention to her son's. Rizpah desires to possess her son— "Flesh of my flesh was gone, but bone of my bone was left" (51)—in strength and spirit. By making him a martyr, she can imagine herself as one; by believing he is saved, she can feel redeemed, too. Symbolically, Rizpah identifies with her son when she describes both her son, who robbed the mail, and herself, who stole the bones from the lawyers, as innocent thieves. Like her son who was "put away" in prison and hanged "in chains for a show" (35–36), Rizpah was put away in a madhouse where she was shamed, brutalized, and dispirited. Rizpah sees herself and her son, unquestioningly, as victims of society. But is "Rizpah" primarily written as a form of social criticism, any more than *Maud* is?

In "Rizpah" as in *Maud*, Tennyson camouflages disturbing love relationships by outwardly criticizing social evils—e.g., Mammonism in *Maud* and Justice in "Rizpah." Of course, it was a literary convention for Victorians to criticize such social evils, much as it was extremely popular to praise such literary types as the good soldier, the loving mother, the ideal child, the noble martyr. This does not mean, however, that Tennyson (who himself lost more than one child and was a witness to madness in his family)[18] subscribed to these sentimental, romanticized, or otherwise psychologically simplistic and absolute representations of vice and virtue. The double nature of Rizpah's maternal love suggests an ambivalence on Tennyson's part about how this mother was to be viewed. On the one hand, since "Rizpah" is a mourning poem, like *In Memoriam*, it would be likely for Tennyson, who mourned so fervently for Arthur Hallam, to empathize with a mother who grieves to the depths of her soul for her son. Like the mourner in *In Memoriam*, who searches nature, reason, and even his dreams for the voice, smile, touch, and presence—corporeal or incorporeal—of his beloved Hallam, Rizpah listens religiously for a voice in the night wind and, with the simple words of a common woman, tries to apotheosize her son, Willy. Similarly, the elegist of *In Memoriam* attempts to turn Hallam into a Christ figure, a hero, a martyr, a redeemer. But unlike the speaker of *In Memoriam* who retains his sanity because he realizes, ultimately, that obsessive mourning, making a "parade of pain" (21:10), is solipsistic, narcissistic, and faithless, Rizpah believes that in collecting her son's bones and listening for her name called in the wind she can "gather [her] baby together" and conquer death. Rizpah's madness results, at least in part, from her not realizing that her unbearable grief for her son is self-reflexive and narcissistic.

Furthermore, in portraying Rizpah with ambivalence, Tennyson shows that obsessional mourning for her son is a method of making Willy more important, loving, and devoted a son to Rizpah in death than he ever was to her in life. In life, Willy was not a hero or martyr or saint, but a spirited and rebellious son who "lived with a lot of wild mates" (29) and who was "whipt" by his mother "for robbing an orchard" (25). Certainly this is a petty crime, but it leads to the more serious crime of robbing the mail, a crime that brought the family dishonor. Willy's behavior indicates that he was no more the perfect child in life than Rizpah was the perfect mother. But after Willy's incarceration and public hanging all of this changes, at least in Rizpah's mind. In fixating on Willy's centrality after he has died, Rizpah simultaneously exaggerates and denigrates the importance of the self, much as the public hanging of Willy made him more important and more ignoble than he had ever been in life. Rizpah simultaneously becomes the most loving, protective, and faithful of all mothers (the way she wishes her real son would have regarded her) and the most guilt-ridden, because she could not save her "baby" from the hangman's noose. Rizpah's idealization of her "baby" is not primarily sentimental: she focuses on the dependent, "baby" Willy to forget about the autonomous Willy, who robbed orchards and "lived with a lot of wild mates." At the same time, she is dependent on what she imagines to be Willy's unremitting love and need for her, feelings she believes so strong that they have bridged life and death. But these idealized feelings of a mother-son relationship are, as we have seen, self-involving. And Rizpah's madness is both a reaction to the feeling of being trapped in an unspeakably unjust society and an attempt to mask any feelings of unexpressed rage she harbors toward her son, a son who through pure recklessness dragged her into a world of social obloquy and emotional exile.

Rizpah's obsessive mourning is not only personally destructive, but also socially dangerous: it is instinctive and irrational, primal and potentially suicidal. The reason most cultures have mourning rituals—and Victorian society turned mourning into an art—[19] is to offset, through catharsis and group sympathy, these primitive, overpowering, and destructive impulses, which on a large scale could threaten civilization. Since the poem is historically set in the eighteenth century when madness was regarded as a serious threat to order, Rizpah's obsessional behavior would not only be regarded as insane, but also as dangerous to society. Similarly, Willy's behavior as a highwayman (despite the fact that he is more "sinned against than sinning") would be considered threatening in a society that was bent on order and the rigidity of its laws, regardless of how unjust those laws might be. Although the eighteenth-century society represented in "Rizpah" is deplorable, from the crucifying lawyers to the madhouse doctors, law and medicine, as socially destructive and protective forces, have a double nature in common with Rizpah's as the Great Mother. Like Rizpah, who religiously protects love, in effect, by "devouring" it, the laws that crucify men and the doctors that torture mad patients have their counterparts, respectively, in the laws that protect civilization from chaos and the doctors who, by the nineteenth century, were making inroads in curing madness.

Since "Rizpah" was written in the nineteenth century but set in the eighteenth, there is a great temptation to read the poem as one that, employing Rizpah as a victim of social evils, cries out for social reforms, such reforms as the Victorians demonstrated in their more lenient treatment of petty criminals and the insane.[20] Along with this useful kind of interpretation, however, goes the even greater temptation to read "Rizpah" as a poem that idealizes the speaker as a Victorian *mater dolorosa* and a spokeswoman for reform. That Rizpah is actually more sane and spiritual than her society is a point of agreement between critics Alder and Kincaid. But Tennyson, in dramatizing Rizpah as both a *mater dolorosa* and a madwoman refusing to accept the reality of death and the anger behind her mourning, paints a more ambiguous portrait of this "mother of sorrows." And that ambiguity extends to the closure of the poem.

The closure of "Rizpah" combines the imagery of mysticism with that of psychosis in such interchangeable ways that, as with "St. Simeon Stylites," one cannot distinguish hallucination from vision. Provoked by the visiting woman's Calvinistic talk of damnation, Rizpah responds, "Do you think I care for *my* soul if my boy be gone to the fire? / I have been with God in the dark" (78–79). One cannot be sure what the speaker means by having been with God in the dark. One is spiritually with God in the dark when one prays, and mystically so when that communication between God and suppliant is shared. Supporting this kind of interpretation, James Kincaid contends that although Rizpah's "grim contest for her son's bones . . . would in itself seem to repudiate all religion," her "having 'been with God in the dark' " implies that she "has found the more basic and real Christianity."[21] While this kind of interpretation is valid if one views Rizpah as a *mater dolorosa* and Christian, it becomes problematic if one considers Rizpah's bone hunting more Druidic than Christian, and her communications with God in the dark psychotic rather than mystical. Since, except for this mentioning of God in the poem, Rizpah has only described being in the dark with her son Willy, it is possible that she has the two confused. Tennyson leaves the answer to this query open-ended since he allows for both possibilities: that Rizpah is intensely religious, more so than anyone else in her society, and that she is mad, and, therefore, unreliable as a spokesperson against social evils.

The same kind of ambiguity is invested in the auditory images of Willy calling Rizpah "now from the church and not from the gibbet" (84) and in the shaking of the walls (85), which that calling produces. A Christian interpretation of the first auditory images would liken Willy to Christ, his voice becoming that of the redeemer after the crucifixion at the gibbet. This kind of reading would follow from the Christian imagery in the poem that has already been alluded to. But this voice in the night may also be an auditory hallucination, like Willy's insistent wailings in the wind, for as Freud writes in *Mourning and Melancholia,* mourning can sometimes become so obsessive and intense that the mourner clings to the lost love-object "through the medium of hallucinatory wishful psychosis."[22] Such a "voice," when apotheosized, would be a sign that Willy, contrary to what the visitor had just said about damnation, was now one of the Elect, and this would mean that Rizpah was also saved from the fire because she had been such a good mother, faithful and vigilant. Analogous to the way St. Simeon Stylites interprets the angel with the "glittering face" (202) to be a clear sign that he is "whole, and clean, and meet for Heaven" (210) because to interpret the sign in any other way would make a complete mockery of his life of abstinence and mortification, Rizpah needs the apotheosized voice to prove to her that the law had, indeed, been brutal, that her suffering had been for a reason, that her boy had transcended death, and that she, by extension, will be reunited with a powerful and forgiving son in death. Since both dramatic monologues focus on anxiety-ridden speakers as they are about to face their deaths, it is perhaps the terror of facing the unknown of death itself that produces these needed "visions" and visitations.

The shaking of the walls that Rizpah experiences immediately after she hears her son call to her is also ambiguous, because the imagery is apocalyptic as well as psychotic. The sonic image of walls shaking, either outside or within the self, is vague but frightening because whatever "it" is that is shaking the walls is incredibly powerful, like an earthquake. If Willy is to be identified as a Christ-figure, then the image may be prophetic and apocalyptic, since walls will shake before the Day of Judgment. Given the corruption of society in "Rizpah" such an interpretation of the image is christologically valid. But since the image of world destruction "equals self-destruction in a psychosis,"[23] the shaking walls, like the commonwealth breaking down in "Lucretius" (241), may also represent what is happening to Rizpah mentally and internally as psychic confusion builds to a maddening pitch. Tennyson allows for both kinds of interpretations by placing the visitor in the same room with Rizpah as she experiences this phenomenon. When Rizpah tells the woman, "Nay—you can hear it yourself—it is coming—shaking the walls—" (5), one recalls Hamlet trying to convince his mother that his father is present and has spoken to him in her bedchamber. One cannot be sure, because the visitor does not respond or react, whether Rizpah is speaking like a madwoman in an asylum or whether hearing the son's Christ-like voice ensures her moral superiority, any more than one can ascertain whether the words Hamlet hears his father speak in his mother's bedchamber are real or hallucinatory.[24]

This kind of ambiguity between vision and hallucination surfaces in psychologically complex ways in "Rizpah" when one is willing to question conventional critical readings of the poem that idealize Rizpah as representing "a quintessential mother love," a *mater dolorosa,* or an innocent victim of social evils and a spokesperson against them. In her obsessive mourning and all-consuming love, Rizpah does not represent an innocent victim of society so much as she personifies an elemental force that finds its counterpart in the duality of creative and destructive forces in the universe. However one interprets the shaking of the walls—as apocalyptic, psychotic, or purely dramatic—it is appropriate that like the dualism of the Great Mother as a life-giver and life-taker, the image of the walls is both creative and destructive. Mythically, the shaking walls, like the fetishistic bones that homeopathically signify both life and death, represent a destructive principle that is inherent in all forms of creation, human as well as architectural. Christologically, shaking walls portend the destruction of cities that will give rise to the New Jerusalem. Anatomically, the shaking of the uterine walls (Rizpah still longs for the baby that once shared her womb) that leads to birth also has a destructive counterpart in the shaking of cranial walls, or of the body, which may precede a cerebral hemorrhage or death. In this case, the shaking walls, like Rizpah's image of bones in her womb, signify birth as well as death. Poetically, the shaking of the walls liberates Rizpah from her prison of despair, and from the poem it self, by allowing her to escape the constraints of Calvinistic reality imposed on her consciousness by the visitor. At the same time that such liberation, mental as well as physical, serves as a defense mechanism, the shaking walls may also be the harbinger of Rizpah's death. The poem ends in uncertainty because one cannot be sure where Rizpah is heading—to the bright downs? to reunion with her son? to sleep? to death? to nothingness?—at the end of the poem. Indeed, when Rizpah finally tells her visitor, "Goodnight. I am going. He calls" (86), not only is the moon "in a cloud" (86), but the closure of the poem, too, is shrouded in ambiguity, leaving the reader's expectations, like the nature of Rizpah's love, in limbo.

Although "Rizpah" ends in ambiguity, it is significant that it is an elemental force in nature that paradoxically devours at the same time that it loves, and not primarily the lamentations of a glorified *mater dolorosa*, that Tennyson vitalizes in "Rizpah." And it is Rizpah's inability to reconcile these dialectical forces (even though she, ironically, represents them in her love for her son and in her mourning) that leads her to mysticism and madness. In writing "Rizpah," therefore, Tennyson not only questions the morality of a society that would hang innocent lads and torment insane women, but also implies that an all-consuming maternity and obsessive mourning, which had been glorified in Victorian literature and society, has a more problematic side, a side that Freud would later explore more fully, with less camouflage, in *Mourning and Melancholia* and *Studies in Hysteria*.

6

"Romney's Remorse"
Pure or Refracted Light on a Canvas?

Each of the four poems previously discussed focuses on characters who lack an autonomous identity and, consequently, try to merge with or disengage from some desired or threatening other. In each of these earlier works, the other is spectral or transient, in addition to being influentially silent. We hear Willy's voice, see Simeon's crown, and behold Lucretius's demons in a phantasmagoria of dreams, fears, and desires; and the more realistic portrait of Maud fades as she disappears into the haunted speaker's selective memory of her. In the final dramatic monologue to be discussed, "Romney's Remorse" (1889), we once again envision the silent auditor, Romney's wife Mary, through the speaker's descriptions of her. Although Romney is under the influence of an opiate as he portrays Mary and speaks to her, his focus is sustained long enough on his wife, and their physical interactions as a couple are realistic enough, for us to consider both characters and their marital situation central to the theme of personal responsibility that shapes this poem. As in "Rizpah," Tennyson once again blends spiritual and secular imagery, but this time to shroud in mystery the questions about art, faith, and marital duty that the poem raises.

"Romney's Remorse," a dramatic monologue about marital infidelity and its consequences, appears to be the most conventional of Tennyson's poems that also deals with the condition of intermittent insanity. Written when Tennyson was eighty years old and recovering from a severe rheumatic illness,[1] which his wife had seen him through, the poem dramatizes Romney's attempts at being remorseful because he had so early abandoned an infant daughter and a saintly wife for "harlot-like Art" (111). In the poem, Romney's wife, Mary Abbot, shows her Christian capacity for charity and forgiveness by nursing her husband through a final illness that has affected his mind. Bordering in places on the sentimental, the poem embraces a number of Victorian literary conventions: the repentant sinner, the forgiving, long-suffering wife, the dead child, the unhappily married artist, and the deathbed confession—complete with tears.

The poem also ostensibly subscribes to the popular Victorian belief that severe illness often had a moral design because it could be the path to humility, contrition, righteousness, forgiveness, and salvation. Many Victorians believed what Jeremy Taylor had written two centuries earlier in *The Rule and Exercises of Holy Dying* (1651)—that "the soul, by the help of sickness, knocks off the fetters of pride and vainer complacencies."[2] In the poem, Romney appears to undergo this process when he stumbles "back again / Into the common day, the sounder self," where "The best of me that sees the worst in me, / And groans to see it, finds no comfort there" (31–32 and 43–44). A Christian reading of "Romney's Remorse," therefore, would uphold Mary Abbot as an instrument of Grace and emphasize the powers of love and illness to redeem a sinner.

While there is ample evidence in "Romney's Remorse" to support such a Christianized reading, there are also tensions in this dramatic monologue between love and guilt that make the Christian resolutions to madness in the poem problematic. These tensions are crystallized in the "dark opiate" (30) that both maddens and cures. That this poem has received so little attention from critics suggests that readers may have oversimplified the poem by narrowly focusing on the qualities of charity, contrition, fidelity, sacrifice, compassion, and forgiveness without considering the dynamics of childlike submission and domination that are inherent in the relationship between Romney and his wife. Tennyson himself wrote of Romney's remorse that he did not know whether the painter actually "did feel it, so I put him under the influence of the opiate, and if you take an opiate without needing it, it acts on your feelings."[3] Having drawn on William Hayley's biography of George Romney (1809), Tennyson would have been aware that the portraitist was a hypochondriac;[4] therefore, the opiate may not have been necessary. Furthermore, if one takes Tennyson at his word, one might question why Mary would give her husband the opiate when Tennyson allows for the possibility that he may not have needed it. Tensions in the poem show that Romney's attitude toward his wife is more ambivalent than a surface reading might indicate.

Romney's implied classifications of his wife as a Madonna and Art as a harlot pose a problem regarding love similar to that seen in Lucretius's conflict with the two Venuses. The kind of love dramatized in this poem, therefore, may not solely, or even primarily, be Christian; furthermore, Romney's role as a repentant sinner and Mary's as the paragon of virtue need to be reconsidered. Indeed, there is darkness as well as light in "Romney's Remorse": the sun does rise, but it flames "along another dreary day" (11. 54–55). Such shadings in the poem are anticipated when Romney questions, and leaves his readers to determine, "What artist ever yet, / Could make pure light live on the canvas?" (9–10). A purely Christian reading of "Romney's Remorse," therefore, has its limitations, for like "the Painter's fame" (42) that Romney describes, the Victorian conventions in this work may be "a coloured bubble" that "bursts above the abyss / Of Darkness" after having been "Blown into glittering by the popular breath" (51–52 and 48).

Philip Henderson has claimed that the marital situation in "Romney's Remorse" is in antithesis to that depicted in "Lucretius" and that Tennyson in the former was expiating his own guilt for having sacrificed his loving wife Emily for art.[5] Although Henderson does not support his position with textual evidence (focusing, instead, on biographical coincidence), such a comparison is useful since Romney's Mary in her maternal and spiritual compassion would appear to be the opposite of Lucilia in her feline and pagan petulance. Furthermore, if one considers Mary's opiate to be the opposite of Lucilia's love philter, one might further classify these women, respectively, as a good nurse and as an Eve-like temptress. But a less traditional application of this comparison is encouraged when one considers the difference in Lucretius's and Romney's sexual natures and needs. The contrasts between Lucilia and Mary may actually demonstrate that Mary would have made a better wife for Lucretius than for Romney. Mary, as "The true Alcestis of the time" (86), recalls Lucretia, whom Lucretius idealizes (235–40), because of her piety, loyalty, and martyrdom to her husband. Lucretius would prefer an "angel in the house," a maternal, sexually nonthreatening, and morally inspiring "Venus," while Romney, not fearful like Lucretius of his animality, was more needful until his illness of a sensual "Venus," epitomized by the Lady Hamilton, whom he never wearied of painting (2–3). While Romney does try to immortalize Mary at the end of his life by painting her (83–93), it is significant that he cannot complete the portrait of her. This is partly because he is feeble and guilt-ridden about his daughter's death (106–7), but it is also because Mary cannot inspire him in the way that a more sensual and less "perfect" woman, like the Lady Hamilton, could. While Mary is fixed in Romney's mind in the roles of mother and wife, the transformational Lady Hamilton triggers Romney's imagination as a fascinating combination of many women in one; she can be Joan and Hebe one minute, and Cassandra and Bacchante the next (4 and 6).

Unlike Mary, who recalls Sara Coleridge in "The Eolian Harp"—

both women have a "more serious eye" that bids their respective husbands away from the "Fairyland" of their imagination—the Lady Hamilton inspires Romney because he can envision and paint her both as saint and sinner, martyr and siren, Christian and pagan. It is perhaps for this reason that Romney in the beginning of the poem hallucinates Lady Hamilton sitting beside him when he suddenly remembers the refrain from his wife's song " 'Beat little heart' " (1–2). If this vision of Lady Hamilton results from a wish-fulfillment, then Romney may be revealing that he unconsciously prefers Lady Hamilton to his wife. Ironically, it is Mary's song that inspires this vision of the Lady Hamilton, which suggests that Romney wants in one person the qualities of womanhood that he envisions, except in art, as mutually exclusive, that of the whore and the Madonna. The Lady Hamilton can suggest both qualities because she is more mythic than motherly; Mary lacks the "infinite variety" of the Lady Hamilton because her sexuality is limited to her roles as childbearer and nurturer.

Only when he is ill does Romney recognize the special comforts of a Madonna, yet it is his illness and not his love that causes Romney to yoke himself to Mary as she takes on the nurturing role of mother rather than wife. In contrast, therefore, to Henderson's premise, if the marital situation in "Romney's Remorse" is more favorable than that depicted in "Lucretius," it is not because Mary is a better wife to Romney than Lucilia is to Lucretius, but because Mary finally becomes beneficial to Romney as a mother. There is additional evidence in the poem that supports the view that Romney, now ill and dependent, would rather be Mary's child than her husband, and, furthermore, that he may have wanted that role when he married her.

While the death of his daughter fills Romney with remorse, he does not seem to mind taking on his infant daughter's role as he is nursed and cradled and sung to by Mary in a lap-side return to mother and child symbiosis. Like a child wanting to retreat to the womb, Romney requests of Mary, "O let me lean my head upon your breast" (147). Romney's regressive desire for lullabies (" 'Beat little heart' ") and other comforts at a mother's breast makes one wonder whether the line "Human forgiveness touches heaven" (152) is also part of a lullaby that could be sung to a child who needed to be soothed in heaven as well as on earth by a Madonna. Therefore, when Romney admits to his wife that he loves her now "more than when we were married" (150), this may not be a genuine sign that he has matured morally and spiritually, but an indication that he has regressed into a state of dependency and submission because of a childlike need to be healed both physically and spiritually.

While this kind of interpretation will not please readers who would like to view "Romney's Remorse" as expressing the same kind of conflict between the artist and marriage as, say, "Andrea del Sarto" does, Romney's love both for Mary and his daughter in this poem is more psychologically complex than "the Master's apothegm, / That wife and children drag an Artist down" (36–37). Even as Mary ministers to him, Romney confesses:

> This Art, that harlot-like
> Seduced me from you, leaves me harlot-like,
> Who love her still, and whimper, impotent
> To win her back before I die. . . .
>
> (110–13)

The passage is ambiguous because Romney wants to win back both his motherly wife and "harlot-like" Art before he dies. By unconsciously displacing the daughter as Mary's child, Romney can now do the former; but like the speaker in "The Palace of Art," he is not content unless he can have both worlds: he wants his "cottage in the vale" ("The Palace of Art," 291) of Kendal, but he does not want his palace of art to be pulled down ("The Palace of Art," 293) by his critics, because he hopes that he may return to it when he has purged himself of guilt ("Palace of Art," 295–96).

Thus far, we have focused primarily on Romney, but Mary, the silent auditor, is too central in this dramatic monologue to be passed over. Because Mary does not speak directly in the poem, one must rely on Romney's (admittedly questionable) responses to her implied words, gestures, and actions to interpret the dynamics of their relationship. On a positive note, Romney refers to his attendant wife's vulnerability and compassion: she nurses her husband's fever with water and tears; her hand trembles; she does her husband "too much grace" (24–27). Perhaps Mary is nurturing Romney in expiation of her failure to save her infant daughter. Whether Mary actually feels responsible for the infant's death, however, is not crucial, because Mary's need to nurture seems almost as strong as Romney's need to be nursed. Conventional readings of the poem, however, would interpret Mary's behavior toward her husband as one of pure altruism, charity, and compassion, whereas she may be in as much need as her husband is. Mary also attempts to play the role of the good mother when she tries to encourage the defeated Romney by telling him to " 'Take comfort you have won the Painter's fame' " (42), and tries to show her forbearance as a wife when she allows Romney to begin a portrait of her—with commands, no less (93)—even though it was

Art in the first place that Romney admits made this "wife of wives a widow-bride" (133). Whether these qualities of compassion and forbearance make Mary an ideal woman or a less-than-ideal martyr and masochist depends on whether one accepts or rejects the Victorian view of the perfect wife as an "angel in the house."

Even if one does accept this view, however, there are several indications in the poem that Mary is not as angelic as she seems. Less to Mary's credit and indicative of the speaker's abiding ambivalence toward her are Romney's references to the "dark opiate dose" she has given him. He says that this dark opiate may have bred his "black mood" (58), a mood that is intensified into hysteria when he accuses Mary of making him insane: "The coals of fire you heap upon my head / Have crazed me" (135–36). Since Romney's reliability as a speaker is made questionable by his "intermittent insanity" (cf. "Lucretius") and by the ambiguous interplay of "lucid intervals" and periods of derangement in the poem, one cannot be sure whether the "coals of fire" he feels are guilt feeilngs, whether he is having a somatic reaction to the "healing" opiate, whether he is paranoid in thinking his wife is poisoning him, or whether the good nurse Mary has a Medea side to her, the result of a repressed rage at having lost a beloved daughter largely because of her husband's negligence.

Along with his preoccupation with the dark opiate, Romney's fixed attention to Mary's bright Christian wedding ring suggests a conflict of emotions. While Romney is fascinated by the sunlight brightness of Mary's wedding ring (35 and 56), he is as much repelled by what it signifies as he is entranced by it. On the one hand, it represents his wife's utter devotion and solicitude to him, but it is also a primary source of guilt (as the dead daughter is), a symbolic reminder of how far he has strayed from a social ideal. Furthermore, Romney cannot help seeing his own darkness reflected in his wife's nunlike brightness. While it is this brightness that Romney hopes will save him (154), it is also this brightness that serves as the worst kind of *unspoken* criticism in the poem.

In addition to Mary's bright Christian wedding ring, her song that echoed in Romney "while I stood / Before the great Madonna-masterpieces / Of ancient Art in Paris, or in Rome" (80–82) is also a source of guilt: it reminds him, before the idealized pictures of Madonnas, of a betrayed duty to his wife and child. The song takes on the voice of his conscience; it makes him long for an alternative self, much as Maud's warlike song not only inspires the protagonist in *Maud,* but also reminds him of how unmanly, how unheroic he has been. Mary's song to her infant daughter becomes less of a haunting echo, less of a reminder of the speaker's parental guilt, when Romney regressively turns it back into a lullaby, but this time for himself. It is as if the only way for Romney to approach and love his perfect, nunlike, Madonna-wife is by becoming her child, nonsexual, submissive, and idealizing. The mother-wife, in turn, must make her child-husband the center of her world, the cause of her existence, the source of her identity. In this dramatic monologue, Mary exists (as Maud does) primarily because Romney needs her. Her role is to nurture, to encourage, to forgive, and to love—and all of this, in silence. Yet, as we have seen, this kind of solicitude and all-forgiving, all-encompassing nurturing may have a darker side. If one interprets Mary as representing an ideal Victorian wife, then one has to question that ideal, especially in a poem that questions the nature of charity, sacrifice, and remorse. In fact, the way the marital relationship is set up in "Romney's Remorse" reminds one of Harriet Taylor's argument in "The Enfranchisement of Women" (1856) that subservient women impoverish rather than enhance a marriage, because when the wife becomes "ancillary," or a "mere appendage" to her spouse, both partners suffer in the furtherance of their identities and ambitions.[6]

Although Tennyson agreed with many of his contemporaries (and, I might add, not a few suffragettes) that women were in general morally and spiritually "much better than men,"[7] he sympathized with Mill and others who promoted the Married Women's Property Act (1870)[8] and advocated women's enfranchisement to correct the inequities in education for men and women. Furthermore, in *The Princess* (1847), Tennyson had anticipated the viewpoint expressed by Taylor and Mill when the Prince says of the bond between husband and wife, "If she be small, slight-natured, miserable, / How shall men grow?" (7.249–50). In addition, as Diane Long Hoeveler argues, we also find in *The Princess* an early representation of the child-husband, mother-wife pattern in Ida's need to mother not only the baby Aglaia, but also the infantilized Prince.[9] While some might find this kind of psychological dependency unusual in poems by Tennyson, symbiotic, narcissistic, and even masochistic dependencies between the sexes are a common conflict, as we can discern in poems ranging from "Fatima," "Mariana," "Oenone," *The Lover's Tale,* and *Maud* to *The Princess, The Idylls of the King,* and "Rizpah."

Perhaps Tennyson was too aware of his public's and critics' cultural needs to question the value of traditional womanhood outright. He did this in *The Princess,* and that is one of the reasons the poem won so little favor among the critics. Tennyson's hypersensitivity to the power of critics to make or break an artist's reputation, even after death, is implicit in what Romney has to say about critics. These fickle evaluators, who can at one turn make an artist's fame glitter with their "popular breath" (47–48) and at the next ruin a reputation with a "loud world's bastard judgment" (114), are for Romney objects of contempt and fear. His view of them as a "mindless mob" implies both this fear and contempt: Romney feels superior to the "mindless mob" because he has gained a name, but he fears the "mob" because he needs the critics to ensure his fame as a superior human being. His simultaneous contempt, fear, and need of the critics' approval make Mary more powerful as a stable source from which he can elicit positive valuation.

A greater source of anxiety than the world's judgment of him is his fear of God's judgment. In his delirium, Romney worries about how he will be judged by Christ and imagines being tormented in Hell by "all the dead" (121–34). It is not surprising that Romney should torment himself with a vision of hell, since, as Erasmus Darwin says, "the most common maniacal hallucination is the fear of hell."[10] While the imagery of the hallucination is infernal, the people Romney describes in hell are variants of the critics who also gibber and point and jeer (131–32) self-righteously. Romney's depiction of hell, there-fore, is an exaggerated view of the critics made grotesque and pitiless. As with the critics, Romney fears this mindless horde of adulterers, wife-murderers, and "ruthless" Mussulmen (128–29), but also has contempt for them since he believes that they have committed bolder sins than his. Furthermore, in Romney's delirium, Mary is complicit with these hellish critics, because Romney, using the imagery of hell, accuses Mary of heaping "coals of fire" upon his head (135). She is therefore perceived as the one who either can save him from the pit of hell or the one who will insure his place there.

Romney is so disturbed by his guilt-ridden vision of hell, the effect of the dark opiate, or his fear of Mary's power over him (probably a combination of the three) that he begins to speak wildly, has an auditory hallucination—"Someone knocking there without?" (136)—and, like the protagonist of *Maud*, imagines himself dead: "Will my Indian brother come? to find / Me or my coffin?" (137–38). He is tortured by the thought that as his body dies, he will lose all powers of reason (139) and not be able to recognize loved ones or speak to them on his deathbed. Therefore, he must depend completely on Mary for positive testimony. A reader who views this poem as a pure expression of Christian compassion, faith, and grace would most likely conclude that Mary will follow her husband's wishes, because she is the "death-bed Angel" that whispers " 'Hope' " (142) and the one from whom the light of forgiveness will be reflected from Heaven "on the forgiven" (154). Given such an interpretation, Romney's illness would, as the Victorians popularly believed, have led to these words of contrition and holy thoughts of salvation.

But the closure of the poem is more ambiguous than this. Romney's "death-bed Angel," like St. Simeon Stylites' angel with the "glittering face" (202), may be a product of delirium or a less than benevolent spirit in disguise. Furthermore, Romney's curious allusion to *Measure for Measure*[11] (143–44) and the tentativeness of his "Hope" allow for divergent conclusions. It is ironic that Romney should quote Claudio's words from *Measure for Measure*—" 'The miserable have no medicine / But only Hope!' He said it . . . in the play"—because Claudio is driven to this medicinal dependency on Hope not so much because of his own sensual nature (almost everyone else in the dukedom is equally lustful), but because his sister Isabella, who resembles Romney's Mary in her nunlike virtue, will not risk her reputation to save her brother from the "region of thick-ribbed ice" (*MM* 3.1.123). Moreover, since *Measure for Measure*, despite its comic resolution, questions the nature of grace, charity, sacrifice, and duty in a realm where sensuality and spirituality are at odds, it is provocative that Tennyson should have Romney quote these words in a poem where harlot-like Art and Madonna-like spirituality are equally divisive. It is also, perhaps, more than coincidental that Romney's message about "Hope" echoes Arthur's last words to Bedivere about the power of prayer in "Morte d'Arthur." In both instances, prayer and Hope would seem to be the optimistic signs of an acceptance of death and the possiblity of renewal in a world where contrition and good deeds can lead to Grace. But in both cases, the speakers, who are dependent on others for their reputations, are uncertain of whether they will be healed, of whether they will be saved. Arthur hopes to go to "the island-valley of Avilion" (259) where "I will heal me of my grievous wound" (264), but he admits to Bedivere, as he drifts away on the "dusky barge," that he is unsure of his destination: "I am going a long way / With these thou seest—if indeed I go— / (For all my mind is clouded with a doubt") (256–58). Romney's mind is also "clouded with a doubt" when he stammers, "O yes, I hope, or fancy that, perhaps, / Human forgiveness touches heaven . . ." (151–52). The tentativeness of these speculative words exhibits Romney's uncertainty about the curative power of Hope and, by extension, the power of his wife's love and the existence of Grace. But because in Romney's mind the alternative to hopefulness is damnation, both by the critics on earth and in hell, he soothes himself into believing that his wife's forgiveness will save him, and that the "death-bed Angel," like St. Simeon's angel, will be a comfort rather than a scourge.

Judging from the tensions in the poem between love and guilt, passion and docility, reason and madness, one can conclude that "Romney's Remorse," while it partakes of the literary conventions of its time (especially that of the curative powers of madness), disturbs those conventions "like a landskip in a ruffled pool" (109). The unreliability of the speaker, as a result of his delirium, and the uncertainty about the nature of Mary's love, because of her dark opiate, free the poem from univocal interpretations that would make it sentimental or cloying for the modern reader. Tennyson's uses of madness in "Romney's Remorse" also keep the poem from being lachrymose and didactic by giving it an ambiguous psychological dimension.

While Tennyson's treatment of madness in "Romney's Remorse" is different than it is in *Maud*, "Lucretius," or "St. Simeon Stylites," it shares some features in common with these earlier poems on madness. For the most part, Tennyson dramatizes Romney as senile rather than as neurotic or psychotic; Romney's grasp on reality is firmer than that of the other speakers and he is not tormented by his animality to the degree that they are. Unlike the protagonist of *Maud* who free-associates by starts and fits throughout the drama, Romney, more like Lucretius, has lucid intervals (e.g., 28–44) and is intermittently insane (e.g., 134–41) when certain words or ideas (e.g., his daughter's death and critical obloquy) disturb him. Because Romney is sedated and one cannot be sure how the opiate is affecting him, it is more difficult at times in this poem than in "Lucretius" to distinguish between a lucid interval and a period of derangement. For instance, when Romney berates both himself and the critics, "Fool, / What matters? Six foot deep of burial mould / Will dull their comments!" (119–21), one cannot be sure whether Romney is in control of his invective or whether his rage has taken control of him to the point that he is no longer aware of his wife's presence. Although Romney's hallucinations of the Lady Hamilton and of hell are less daring and vivid (perhaps because he is sedated and not sexually repressed) than St. Simeon's dream of Abaddon and Asmodeus and Lucretius's nightmares about the hetairai and the flaming breasts of Helen, these hallucinations are appropriate to the kind of more settled nature that Romney has had in life. He worries about guilt, so he envisions the punishments of hell; he longs for the Lady Hamilton, so he imagines she is beside him rather than his wife (2). But like St. Simeon Stylites, the narrator of *Maud*, Lucretius, and Rizpah, Romney is fixated on certain images and ideas, for instance, his wife's song, his daughter's death, the bright Christian wedding ring, and the slandering critics. There are other vestiges of "St. Simeon Stylites," "Lucretius," and *Maud* in "Romney's Remorse" that indicate that the later poem springs from the earlier ones, even though it is more conventional. For instance, the refrain " 'Beat, little heart,' " which brings Romney back to consciuosness, reminds one of the unexpected phrase " 'The fault was mine,' " which opens section 2 of *Maud*. In both cases the refrain is a product of guilt based on a past event: the duel with Maud's brother in *Maud* and the death of the infant daughter in "Romney's Remorse." And, as we have already seen, Mary's dark opiate finds its counterpart in Lucilia's love philter.

In addition to dramatizing another form of madness in "Romney's Remorse," Tennyson manages to target a problem intrinsic to marital relationships through the indirection of the dramatic monologue. It is because Mary does not speak directly to the reader that her value as an "angel in the house" can be disputed. Because Romney speaks for his wife, there is no way, for instance, to ascertain whether Mary's tone is sincere or ironic when she tells her husband to "take comfort, you have won the Painter's fame" (42), especially in a poem in which the speaker believes he has "lost / Salvation for a sketch" (133–34). Similarly, one cannot confirm whether Mary is a good nurse trying to heal her husband or an avenging angel "heaping coals" of revenge upon his head for a daughter's death, any more than one can prove whether the "death-bed Angel" is a benevolent spirit or a malevolent product of the speaker's delirium. That both interpretations are possible indicates Tennyson was offering a mixed view in "Romney's Remorse" about the benefits of wifely solicitude[12] and the healing powers of contrition that emerge from guilt. Although Tennyson paints what would appear at the surface to be a picture of abiding love and sacrifice as bright, sacred, and inviolable as Mary's Christian wedding ring, there are also shadows on the canvas that reveal Tennyson's portrait of marriage in the poem to be more gray, less traditional. The bifurcation in "Romney's Remorse" of Madonna and harlot discloses that a mother-wife (like Mary) can *create* a child-husband (like Romney) as well as cure him, because of overindulgence; furthermore, a child-husband can easily abandon his sexless Madonna for a more sensual woman, like the Lady Hamilton. The delayed reward for the abandoned mother-wife will be the return of the child-husband when he, hobbling, whimpering, and impotent, needs to be dependent on his wife's maternal rather than sexual love. Therefore, for all its sentiment and all its glow of altruism, "Romney's Remorse" does not uphold Mary Abbot as a paragon of virtue any more than it does Romney as a great painter. Mary's fame as a martyr-wife, like Romney's "Painter's fame," is "Blown into glittering by the popular breath." And as history has shown, such angelic fame in a woman or public acclaim for an artist "May float awhile beneath the sun, may roll / The rainbow hues of heaven about it" (48–49), until it bursts "above the abyss / Of darkness, utter Lethe" (51–52).

Conclusion

As the poems discussed in the preceding chapters of this book demonstrate, Tennyson's keen observations on madness are remarkable in that the poet not only utilized but also saw beyond and challenged the more repressive cultural values of his age. Although Ann C. Colley contends in *Tennyson and Madness* that Tennyson "shared in the public's fear that England and its subjects had become slaves to their passions,"[1] the poems treated suggest an alternative view: that Tennyson saw unbridled passion and madness not as the cause but as the effect of social expectations and moral pressures that were too rigid in their prohibitions of desire and other forms of self-expression, including artistic expression. Criticizing this rigidity, Tennyson links madness in each poem to the feeling of surveillance and consequent judgment or persecution by silent "others." St. Simeon Stylites is spiritually terrified because he fears the final judgment of a fathering God; Lucretius's sexual paranoia leads to the tortured belief that he is being pursued by prostitutes and satyrs; the protagonist of *Maud* believes everything he whispers is being "shouted from the rooftops" by a society he feels is vile, treacherous, and degenerate; Rizpah believes the charity worker (and the whole town) is spying on her as she listens for Willy's phantom voice in the night wind; Romney fears that his critics are preparing a pit in hell for him. Because the speakers also seek the approval of the "others," and because of the fine balance Tennyson achieves between criticism and sympathy for these speakers, their paranoid reactions must not only be read as a sign of their individual pathology, but also as an indicator of the social pressures that triggered those reactions.

A close reading of these poems also confirms that Tennyson could portray abnormal states of the mind with more drama, stylistic complexity, and psychological accuracy than some critics have allowed. William E. Fredeman, who is representative of the many critics that favor Robert Browning's dramatic monologues to Tennyson's, argues that Tennyson's monologists fall short in their dramatic and psychological interest because they are totally introspective, unable to act, or even paralyzed.[2] On the contrary, in these poems, the paralysis of physical action is more than compensated for by the kinesis of mental

114

action. Lucretius, for instance, may not actively participate in the chase between the satyr and the Oread, but his mind is the landscape of that frantic chase with all of its erotic tensions. Furthermore, if the speakers are rendered physically powerless, it is because they are "other-directed": their fame, purpose in life, or will to live is dependent on silent witnesses; therefore, it is the symbiotic relationship between the self and the "other" in these poems that sustains the psychological tension. Unlike Browning, who is undoubtedly masterful at creating aggressive psychological characters, Tennyson most often makes his mad monologists the victims of others' expectations and judgments rather than the controllers. As Carol T. Christ rightly summarizes, "While Browning's characters engage themselves in a mad projection of the will to manipulate the world, Tennyson's characters typically fear that any attempt to engage the world will meet with blank unrecognition, absolute otherness."[3] Browning's Johannes Agricola, his Duke in "My Last Duchess," and his murderers in "Porphyria's Lover" and *The Ring and the Book* are all monomaniacs who use their obsessions aggressively to gain power or to keep from "stooping." Conversely, Tennyson's mad monologists are terrified of being rejected, of going insane, of losing control, of being alienated, of not being loved. Although Tennyson's speakers are instinctively aggressive, they have much less rhetorical confidence and bravado than Browning's mad monologists do. In addition, their hypertrophied consciences make Tennyson's speakers invariably more masochistic than Browning's, since they punish themselves for having desire.

Tennyson's intuitive awareness of the hypertrophied conscience and its masochistic component links poems like "St. Simeon Stylites" and *Maud* to "The Love Song of J. Alfred Prufrock"—in which there is also the dread of social ostracism. Prufrock's excessive self-consciousness, his problem with desire, and his neurotic vacillations in self-esteem are on a par with those of Tennyson's mad characters. As Carol T. Christ notes, Prufrock, like Tennyson's monologists, is confined to his "solitary ego" because he doubts "that there can be meaningful interchange between the world and the self."[4] Perhaps in writing such poems, Tennyson was also questioning how much of a meaningful interchange there could be between the artist and his world.

T. S. Eliot aptly observed that Tennyson was "the most instinctive rebel against the society in which he was the most perfect conformist."[5] If such a division did exist, one could speculate that it was between Tennyson's need for public approbation and his desire for autonomy as an artist. As the arbiters of public taste, Victorian critics strongly encouraged the kind of poetry that would edify the public,[6] and Tennyson was strongly criticized when he deviated from these expectations by writing experimental poems, like *The Princess* and *Maud*. Such criticism would probably have rolled off the back of an iconoclast like Swinburne, but Tennyson's need to conform corresponded with his hypersensitivity to criticism. According to James Knowles, Tennyson

> could never forget an unfriendly word, even from the most obscure and unknown quarter. He was hurt by it as a sensitive child might be hurt by the cross look of a passing stranger; or rather as a supersensitive skin is hurt by the sting of a midge.[7]

Furthermore, such insecurity about criticism and, therefore, about his own self-worth, would have compelled Tennyson to seek approbation outside of himself. In a letter to his friend Edward FitzGerald, Tennyson sounds like Romney beseeching Mary when he writes,

> . . . don't you know that I esteem you one of those friends who will stick to me though the whole polite world with its great idiot mouth . . . howled at me. . . .[8]

While the tone of this letter is uncharacteristic—Tennyson is usually more diplomatic and guarded in his correspondence—the letter is important as an exception to the rule because Tennyson does not repress his anger, contempt, or fear in it; rather, he exposes them— cold on the page—to a lifelong friend. Tennyson implies in this letter that close friendship is his protection against a society that he regards as judgmental, potentially hostile, and hypocritical. The hypocrisy of a society bent on decorum resounds in the phrase "the whole polite world with its great idiot mouth." The hypocritically "polite" world is the domain of the charity worker in "Rizpah," and the "great idiot mouth" of the world with its awful howling parallels both the "idiot babble" that the protagonist hears all around him in the third section of *Maud* and the "loud world's bastard judgment" that Romney fears and condemns in "Romney's Remorse."

This is not to say that Tennyson's dissatisfactions with "polite" society and with his critics was excessive or irrational, but it is to suggest that Tennyson's fear of being victimized by critics who could either ensure his fame or cripple it finds an outlet in the mad poems. In each of these poems, a conflict with judgmental authority is magnified to the level of obsession. The speakers' varied attempts to create, destroy, or re-create Gods, love ideals, or familial situations replicate the psychological conflict that occurs when the self first discovers that the mysterious "other" is both a part that it wants to remain attached to and a part that it instinctively wants to reject. This is because the speakers, who are largely narcissistic—they want everything in the world to take on the image of their mind or heart—desire both to remain linked to powerful, influential, and nurturing others, and to remain unique, central, and therefore faithful to their private visions of the world. As an artist, Tennyson's submission to public expectations was naturally at odds with his artistic desire to create visions that were not restricted by rigid moral codes. The need for mass approval from his society compelled the poet laureate to placate his audiences by catering, most often, to the public taste. However, in these poems on madness, Tennyson was able to do something that his mad speakers could not do: he could rationally and subliminally pacify the authorities of his "polite world" while simultaneously coding for them in the art they commissioned from him a blueprint of his dissent.

Notes

Introduction

1. Ann C. Colley, *Tennyson and Madness* (Athens: University of Georgia Press, 1983); Robert B. Martin, *Tennyson: The Unquiet Heart* (Oxford: Clarendon Press, 1980); Harold Nicolson, *Tennyson: Aspects of His Life Character and Poetry* (London: Constable and Company, 1923); E. D. H. Johnson, *The Alien Vision of Victorian Poetry* (1952; reprint, Hamden, Conn.: Archon Books, 1963); Ralph Rader, *Tennyson's Maud: The Biographical Genesis* (Berkeley: University of California Press, 1963); Roy P. Basler, *Sex, Symbolism, and Psychology in Literature* (New Brunswick, N.J.: Rutgers University Press, 1948); Charles Tennyson and Hope Dyson, *The Tennysons: Background to Genius* (London: Macmillan, 1974).

2. My position differs from that of Colley, *Tennyson and Madness*, p. 92, who attributes the madness of Tennyson's speakers mostly to excesses of passion, like monomania. It also differs with Carol T. Christ's tenable view, *Victorian and Modern Poetics* (Chicago: University of Chicago Press, 1984), pp. 5, 8, 17, 19, and 50, that alienation in Tennyson's dramatic monologues is a Victorian warning against the kinds of self-imposed prisons that Romantic solipsism can construct. Although the Victorians did fear Romantic excesses of the imagination, because they could lead to self-enclosure, the "warden" for that prison of the self in the Victorian age was society. In cases of madness, social causation is as responsible for the pathology as is inheritance or individual eccentricity, and Victorian psychiatrists were interested in these cultural determinants.

3. Michel Foucault, *Madness and Civilization: A History of Insanity in the Age of Reason*, trans. Richard Howard (New York: Vintage Books, 1965), p. 289. Andrew T. Scull, ed., *Madhouses, Mad-Doctors, and Madmen: The Social History of Psychiatry in the Victorian Era* (Philadelphia: University of Pennsylvania Press, 1981).

4. The Victorians believed that sexual indulgences, including masturbation, could lead to insanity. For a full discussion of this subject, see Steven Marcus, *The Other Victorians* (New York: Basic Books, 1966), pp. 2, 17, 31, 98, and 245.

5. For a discussion of the relationship between "centrality" (the feeling of being at the center of others' interests and judgments) and paranoia, see David W. Swanson, M.D., Philip J. Bohnert, M.D., and Jackson A. Smith, M.D., *The Paranoid* (Boston: Little, Brown and Company, 1970), p. 15.

6. Robert Langbaum, *The Poetry of Experience: The Dramatic Monologue in Modern Literary Tradition* (London: Chatto and Windus, 1957), pp. 78, 85, and 146.

7. Dorothy Mermin, *The Audience in the Poem: Five Victorian Poets* (New Brunswick, N.J.: Rutgers University Press, 1983), p. 9.

8. Sartre's theory of the "reflector" is mentioned by Leo Bersani in *Baudelaire and Freud* (Berkeley: University of California Press, 1977), p. 112. I have adapted Sartre's term in applying it to the silent auditors in Tennyson's dramatic monologues on madness.

9. Lacan's "mirror stage" is defined and illustrated in *Ecrits: A Selection*, by Jacques Lacan, trans. Alan Sheridan (New York: W. W. Norton and Co., 1977; Paris; Editions du Seuil, 1966), pp. 1–7.

10. Swanson, Bohnert, and Smith, *The Paranoid*, p. 125.

Chapter 1. "Hidden Wells of Scorching Fire"

1. Christopher Ricks, ed., *The Poems of Tennyson* (London: Longmans, Green, and Co., 1969), 2. 4. 94, p. 39. This is the edition used for all line references to Tennyson's poetry. Hereafter, all subsequent part and line references to Tennyson's poems are cited parenthetically in the text.

2. Ricks, *The Poems of Tennyson*, Chronological Tables, p. xxix.

3. Diana Basham, "Tennyson and His Fathers: The Legacy of Manhood in Tennyson's Poems," *Tennyson Research Bulletin* 4 November 1985): 164.

4. Ann C. Colley, *Tennyson and Madness* (Athens: University of Georgia Press, 1983), pp. 16 and 38–44.

5. Cecil Y. Lang and Edgar F. Shannon, Jr., eds., *The Letters of Alfred Lord Tennyson*, Vol. 1: 1821–1850 (Cambridge, Mass.: Belknap Press, 1981), p. 30; see also pp. xx, 14, and 45.

6. Ricks, *The Poems of Tennyson*, p. xxix.

7. Colley, *Tennyson and Madness*, p. 76.

8. Sigmund Freud, *Civilization and Its Discontents*, ed. James Strachey (New York: W. W. Norton, 1961), p. 29.

9. For an interesting discussion of the meanings of Julian's fantasies in "The Lover's Tale," see Herbert F. Tucker, Jr., "Tennyson's Narrative of Desire: 'The Lover's Tale,'" *Victorian Newsletter* 62 (1982): 21–30.

10. Schopenhauer is quoted in Henri F. Ellenberger, *The Discovery of the Unconscious* (New York: Basic Books, 1970), pp. 208–9.

11. R. D. Laing, *The Divided Self* (New York: Pantheon Books, p. 160), p. 45.

12. Critics generally see the dramatic monologue as having developed out of prosopopoeia, or the rhetorical form in which a historical figure speaks on an occasion. For a useful summary of theories on the dramatic monologue and their implications, see Carol Christ, *Victorian and Modern Poetics* (Chicago: University of Chicago Press, 1984), pp. 26–27. In addition to the items mentioned in Christ's summary, I think the relationship between the dramatic monologue and the traditional psychomachia could be explored by critics.

Chapter 2. "St. Simeon Stylites"

1. Although a number of critics have alluded to Simeon as mentally unstable, they have not made madness or its Victorian topicality the chief issue in this poem. For instance, Robert Langbaum, *The Poetry of Experience: The Dramatic Monologue in Modern Literary Tradition* (London: Chatto and Windus, 1957), p. 87, writes that St. Simeon's "hallucinations, self-loathing and insatiable lust for self-punishment suggest a psyche as diseased (we should nowadays call it sadomasochistic) as the ulcerous flesh he boasts of." Langbaum adds, "Tennyson pursues the saint's passion to its obscure sexual recesses." David Shaw, *Tennyson's Style* (Ithaca: Cornell University Press, 1976), p. 194, briefly describes Simeon's anality and sadomasochistic impulses, but sees these factors as indicting Simeon rather than humanizing him. Herbert F. Tucker, Jr., "From Monomania to Monologue: 'St. Simeon Stylites' and the Rise of the Victorian Monologue," *Victorian Poetry* 22 (1984): 128, states that

"Simeon's multiple betweenness, the overdetermined and derivative status of his questionable 'I' establishes character in this seminal dramatic monologue as inherently unstable," but Tucker does not explore that instability psychologically.

2. Helen B. Lewis, *Shame and Guilt in Neurosis* (New York: International Universities Press, 1971), p. 104, describes the "field-dependent perceiver" as a person who relies on the approval of others for self-esteem and a stable identity and who is prone to "self-directional hostility."

3. Michel Foucault, *Madness and Civilization: A History of Insanity in the Age of Reason,* trans. Richard Howard (New York: Vintage Books, 1965), p. 20.

4. Lewis, *Shame and Guilt in Neurosis,* p. 194, uses William James's phrase "argumentative internal colloquies" to describe the kinds of psychic battles that occur in neurotics.

5. Lewis, *Shame and Guilt in Neurosis,* p. 194, discusses William James's theory of the "ideal spectator."

6. Dorothy Mermin, *The Audience in the Poem: Five Victorian Poets* (New Brunswick, N.J.: Rutgers University Press, 1983), p. 21, argues that while Simeon cannot trust his heavenly audience, because he "has had enough experience of supernatural responses, . . . to make him wary of colloquy with the divine," Simeon accepts the approval of the earthly crowd as "definitive." Mermin bases this on the assumption that Simeon is dramatic but sane.

7. Tennyson alludes to *Hamlet* in many of his poems. For instance, many of the protagonist's lines in *Maud,* which Tennyson called his "little *Hamlet*," echo the words of Shakespeare's prince. It is also important that before the Victorian period, Hamlet's "derangement was universally regarded as feigned," but because Victorian psychiatrists had secularized religious visions into hallucinations, the possibility of considering the relationship between visions and hallucinations, as in *Hamlet* (and, by extension, in "St. Simeon Stylites"), developed in studies of insanity. Isaac Ray, *Contributions to Mental Pathology: Facsimile Reproduction,* with an introduction by Jacques M. Quen (1873; reprint, New York: Scholars Facsimiles and Reprints, 1973), p. 504.

8. This is one point upon which Victorian psychiatrists seem to agree. Excessive self-consciousness or morbid introspection, as exemplified in many nineteenth-century psychiatric texts by Hamlet, could lead to forms of derangement, such as the religious melancholia from which St. Simeon Stylites suffers. Henry Maudsley, *The Pathology of Mind* (1895; reprint, London: Julian Friedmann Publishers, 1979), pp. iii and 72, writes, "He who is eternally contemplating his own feelings can scarcely be pronounced to be perfectly sane"; "an excessive self-consciousness is the sorest of human affections."

9. George Man Burrows, *Commentaries on the Causes, Forms, Symptoms, and Treatment, Moral and Medical, of Insanity* (1828; reprint, New York: Arno Press, 1976), pp. 13, 113, 123, and 128, discusses the relationship between changes in blood circulation and mental derangement. John Haslam, *Observations on Madness and Melancholia* (1809; reprint, New York: Arno Press, 1976), p. 67, offers case studies on somatic causes of derangement, e.g., auditory hallucinations. Henry Maudsley, *Body and Will: Being an Essay Concerning Will in its Metaphysical, Physiological, and Pathological Aspects* (New York: D. Appleton and Co., 1884), p. 262, and *The Pathology of Mind,* p. 478, focuses on the somatic causes of epilepsy and describes it as being a form of inherited madness. These are just a few of the hundreds of works that were written on somatic disturbance in the nineteenth century. For an overview of Victorian beliefs on madness and a helpful bibliography, see Ann C. Colley, *Tennyson and Madness* (Athens: University of Georgia Press, 1983), pp. 10–33, and notes throughout.

10. Pinel, *A Treatise on Insanity,* trans. D. D. Davis (1806; reprint, New York: Hafner Publishing Co., 1962), p. 73. See also pp. 113–14.

11. George Man Burrows is quoted by Vieda Skultans in *Madness and Morals: Ideas on Insanity in the Nineteenth Century* (London: Routledge and Kegan Paul, 1975), p. 38.

12. Colley, *Tennyson and Madness,* p. 12.

13. This quotation from Hazlitt is cited and examined in Elisabeth Jay, *The Religion of the Heart: Anglican Evangelism in the Nineteenth-Century Novel* (Oxford: Clarendon Press, 1979), p. 56.

14. T. S. Eliot, *Murder in the Cathedral* (New York: Harcourt, Brace, and World, 1935), p. 38.

15. James R. Kincaid, *Tennyson's Major Poems: The Comic and Ironic Patterns* (New Haven: Yale University Press, 1975), pp. 47–48.

16. William E. Fredeman compares Simeon to Napoleon and other diabolical overreachers in " 'A Sign betwixt the Meadow and the Cloud': The Ironic Apotheosis of Tennyson's St. Simeon Stylites," *University of Toronto Quarterly* 38 (1969): 80.

17. Christopher Ricks, *The Brownings: Letters and Poetry* (New York: Doubleday, 1970), 11. 33–37, p. 321.

18. William Hone, *The Every Day Book* (London: William Tegg and Co., 1878), 1:19.

19. Lewis, *Shame and Guilt in Neurosis,* quotes Nietzsche, p. 44.

20. Although Tennyson could not have been aware of Freud's theory that wild beasts in a dream usually symbolize "passionate impulses," the libido, feared by the ego, and combated by repression, and "the totemistic representation of the dreaded father" (A. A. Brill, ed., *The Basic Writings of Sigmund Freud* [New York: Modern Library, 1938], p. 401), he would have been aware of the long tradition in Western civilization of using the imagery of beasts, for instance in *The Changeling* and *King Lear,* to represent states of madness.

21. Robert Whytt's profile of "Hypochondriacal and Hysterical Affections" is cited by Foucault, *Madness and Civilization,* p. 137.

22. For Freud's theory of conversion hysterias, see Brill, *Basic Writings of Sigmund Freud,* pp. 573 and 934.

23. "Dissolvent literature" refers to works that caused the validity of the Bible and other religious texts to be questioned. During the Victorian period there is a plethora of such works, including Lyell's *Principles of Geology,* Strauss's *Life of Jesus,* Colenso's *Critical Examination of the Pentateuch,* and Darwin's *Origin of Species.*

24. Michael Timko, in "The Victorianism of Victorian Literature," *New Literary History* 6 (1974–75), describes epistemological despair as one of the salient issues in all Victorian literature. He writes, " 'Who am I?' is the great Victorian question; and it can easily be translated into the simpler question 'Am I?' in a time when the assumptions of both Descartes and Wordsworth have to be doubted" (p. 625).

25. W. H. Gardner and N. H. Mackensie, *The Poems of Gerard Manley Hopkins* (London: Oxford University Press, 1967), 11. 2 and 44, pp. 32–33.

26. Ian Bradley, *The Call to Seriousness: The Evangelical Impact on the Victorians* (London: Jonathan Cape, 1976), p. 23.

27. Most recently, Ann C. Colley has argued that Tennyson subscribed "to his contemporaries' preoccupation with the absolute necessity of exercising . . . repression if they and their nation were to be sane." *Tennyson and Madness,* p. 117. As I have shown in this study, the converse may be equally valid or worthy of further thought.

28. Brian Harrison, "Underneath the Victorians," *Victorian Studies* 10 (1966–67): 239–62; Steven Marcus, *The Other Victorians* (New York: Basic Books, 1966), pp. 2,

17, 31, 98, and 245; Elaine and English Showalter, "Victorian Women and Menstruation," *Victorian Studies* 14 (1970–71): 83–89. Although this view of Victorian ignorance and fear of sexuality has been recently challenged in Peter Gay's book *Education of the Senses,* Gay primarily uses diaries or "private writings" to make his case, and the majority of his women surveyed are American rather than British. The evidence of "private writings," however, does not invalidate the provisos against sexual indulgence and the prorepression documents that are everywhere apparent in nineteenth-century "public" writings.

29. Matthew Allen, M.D., *Cases of Insanity* (London: George Swire and H. Bellerby, 1831), p. 60.

30. Carter is quoted in Ilza Veith, *Hysteria: The History of the Disease* (Chicago: University of Chicago Press, 1965), p. 119.

31. William Acton warned parents to watch their children, because sexual indulgences, like masturbation, could lead to mental aberrations. Marcus, *The Other Victorians,* pp. 4, 17, 19, 24, 31, 242–44.

32. Michel Foucault, *The History of Sexuality,* Vol. *1, An Introduction,* trans. Robert Hurley (New York: Random House, 1978), p. 45.

33. John Coulson, ed., *The Saints: A Concise Biographical Dictionary* (New York: Hawthorn Books, 1958), p. 400.

34. John Stuart Mill, *On Liberty,* ed. Currin V. Shields (Indianapolis: Bobbs-Merrill Co., 1956), p. 60.

35. Robert Langbaum has called "St. Simeon Stylites" "a conventional liberal Protestant's attack upon asceticism" (p. 146).

Chapter 3. *Maud*

1. Christopher Ricks, *The Poems of Tennyson* (London: Longmans, Green, and Co., 1969), p. 1039.

2. Ibid. Tennyson reveals a different attitude to the martial ending of *Maud* in a letter to Archer Gurney. See note 28, below.

3. This plot outline, which Ricks does not include in his introductory notes to *Maud,* is taken from Hallam Tennyson, *Alfred Lord Tennyson: A Memoir by His Son* (1897; reprint, New York: Greenwood Press, 1969), 1:394–95. The plot outline is discussed in James R. Bennett, "The Historical Abuse of Literature: Tennyson's 'Maud: A Monodrama' and the Crimean War," *English Studies* 62 (1981): 42.

4. For an enlightening discussion of this Victorian preoccupation with hereditary madness, and its historical antecedents, see Ann C. Colley, *Tennyson and Madness* (Athens: University of Georgia Press, 1983), pp. 16–24.

5. The most thorough treatment of this biographical subject is offered by Robert Barnard Martin in *Tennyson: The Unquiet Heart* (Oxford: Clarendon Press, 1980), pp. 10–25, passim. See also Ann C. Colley, *Tennyson and Madness;* E. D. H. Johnson, *The Alien Vision of Victorian Poetry* (1952; reprint, Hamden, Conn.: Archon Books, 1963); and Ralph Wilson Rader, *Tennyson's Maud: The Biographical Genesis* (Berkeley: University of California Press, 1963).

6. Colley, *Tennyson and Madness,* p. 32.

7. Henry Maudsley, *The Pathology of Mind* (1895; reprint, London: Julian Friedmann Publishers, 1979), quotes the following lines from Maud to characterize melancholia: "Ah what shall I be at fifty / Should Nature keep me alive, / If I find the world so bitter / When I am twenty-five?" (1:220–24). Joseph Adams's book is mentioned by Colley, p. 16.

8. Colley, *Tennyson and Madness,* pp. 23–27.

9. The narrator of *Maud* refers three times to the "spleen" (1:87, 88, and 363), calling himself in the last instance, "splenetic, personal, base." Since "spleen" has a very long medical history, this is one case in the poem where Tennyson's treatment of madness is very conventional. But while the narrator of *Maud* has some of the classic symptoms of the spleen—terrible dreams, sudden fits of anger, and great attention to one object—his defensive kinds of idealization and narcissism transcend the boundaries of humoural pathology and anticipate Freudian nonrational causation in psychosis and dementia. For additional symptoms of the spleen and an informative study of it, see Vieda Skultans, *English Madness: Ideas on Insanity* (London: Routledge and Kegan Paul, 1979), pp. 27–30.

10. The literary influences on *Maud* of such works as *The Bride of Lammermoor, Hamlet, Romeo and Juliet, Alton Locke,* and the two "spasmodic" poems "A Life Drama," by Alexander Smith, and "Balder," by Sydney Dobell, are summarized in Paul Turner, *Tennyson* (London: Routledge and Kegan Paul, 1976), pp. 138–40. For a discussion of operatic rhythmic patterns in *Maud* and the use of recitativo and arias to promote the action and reveal mood changes, see F. E. L. Priestley, *Language and Structure in Tennyson's Poetry* (London: André Deutsch, 1975), p. 118. For a study of other different kinds of voices and mood swings in *Maud,* as well as a treatment of how *Maud* follows the pattern of monodramas in its time, see A. Dwight Culler, "Monodrama and the Dramatic Monologue," *PMLA* 90(1975): 366–85.

11. Ricks, *The Poems of Tennyson,* p. 1039.

12. Christopher Ricks, *Tennyson* (New York: Collier Books, 1972), p. 249.

13. Karl Abraham, *On Character and Libido Development: Six Essays* (New York: Basic Books, 1966), p. 105.

14. Ricks, *The Poems of Tennyson,* p. 1039.

15. These moods of mind are considered by Henry Maudsley in *The Pathology of Mind,* p. 127.

16. Matthew Allen, *Cases of Insanity,* pt. 1, vol. 1 (London: George Swire, 1831), pp. 49 and 53.

17. Maudsley, *The Pathology of Mind,* p. 133, cites this quotation in tracing the history of melancholia.

18. Ronald Weiner, "The Chord of Self: Tennyson's *Maud,*" *Psychology and Literature* 16 (1966): 176.

19. For a definition of *idealization* as a defense mechanism, see Charles Rycroft, *A Critical Dictionary of Psychoanalysis* (Totowa, N.J.: Littlefield, Adams and Co., 1973), p. 67.

20. While critics like Paul Turner have compared *Maud* to *Hamlet* and *Romeo and Juliet,* the incest theme in the three works, to my knowledge, has not been treated. Ernest Jones has made famous the case of Oedipal anxiety and incest in *Hamlet.* But there also seems to be an archetypal form of incest anxiety operating in *Romeo and Juliet* not only between Juliet and Tybalt, but also in the tribal necessity for dividing the Capulet and Montague families into oppositional clans. The conflict between *eros* and *thanatos* in *Romeo and Juliet* is also apparent, especially in the burial-chamber scene that ends the play.

21. Weiner, "The Chord of Self," pp. 177–78.

22. Elisabeth Kübler-Ross, *On Death and Dying* (New York: Macmillan Publishing Co., 1969), p.4, discusses this problem of mourning.

23. Weiner, "The Chord of Self," p. 172.

24. Ricks, *Tennyson,* p. 251.

25. Jonas Spatz, "Love and Death in Tennyson's *Maud,*" *Texas Studies in Literature and Language* 16 (1974–75): 508.

26. Frank Giordano, Jr., "The 'Red-Ribbed Hollow,' Suicide and Part III in 'Maud,'" *Notes and Queries* 24 (1977): 402, refers to the Oedipal blurrings between Maud's brother and the speaker's father in this passage.

27. Henry Maudsley, M.D. *Body and Will* (New York: D. Appleton and Co., 1884), 297.

28. According to Martin, *The Unquiet Heart*, p. 236, "through his friendship with Dr. Matthew Allen, Tennyson was to learn most of what he knew of madness, which looms so large in *Maud*." Ann C. Colley, *Tennyson and Madness*, p. 47, describes how Tennyson met at Malvern "nervous hypochondriacs, hysterics, alcoholics, and those with suicidal longings" (cf. *Maud*, 2:268–78).

29. George Man Burrows, *Commentaries on the Causes, Forms, Symptoms, and Treatment, Moral and Medical, of Insanity* (1828; reprint, New York: Arno Press, 1976), p. 344.

30. Robert Mann is quoted by Ricks in *Tennyson*, p. 162.

31. Ricks quotes the laureate in *Tennyson*, p. 261.

32. Turner, *Tennyson*, cites this letter to Archer Gurney, p. 142. Turner's sources are Richard Andrews, who showed Turner the letter, and Gerald Gurney, who gave his permission to use it.

33. Roy P. Basler, *Sex, Symbolism, and Psychology in Literature* (New Brunswick, N.J.: Rutgers University Press, 1948), p. 87.

34. For a discussion of Tennyson's preoccupation with *Maud* and his hypersensitivity to criticisms directed at the poem, see Ralph Wilson Rader, *Tennyson's Maud: The Biographical Genesis* (Berkeley: University of California Press, 1963), pp. 1–7.

35. Ricks, *Tennyson*, p. 246.

Chapter 4. "Lucretius"

1. "Epistemophilia" is defined in Charles Rycroft, *A Critical Dictionary of Psychoanalysis* (Totowa, N.J.: Littlefield, Adams, and Co., 1973), p. 45.

2. Charles Tennyson, *Alfred Tennyson* (New York: Macmillan Co., 1949), p. 374.

3. This is one of the significant differences between Tennyson's poem and Lucretius's, resulting from the different historical attitudes toward sexuality. To read about some of the many ways in which the poems are alike in phraseology, atmosphere, and characterization, see Ortha Wilner, "Tennyson and Lucretius," *Classical Journal* 25 (1930): 348, 366.

4. Lucertius, *De rerum natura*, trans. W. H. D. Rouse (1937, Loeb Classical Library; reprint, Cambridge: Harvard University Press, 1966) p. 335.

5. George Man Burrows, *Commentaries on the Causes, Forms, Symptoms, and Treatment, Moral and Medical, of Insanity* (1828; reprint, New York: Arno Press, 1976), p. 128.

6. Burrows, *Commentaries*, p. 275.

7. "Periodic" or "intermittent insanity" is discussed in Richard Hunter and Ida Macalpine, *Three Hundred Years of Psychiatry, 1535–1860: A History Presented in Selected English Texts* (London: Oxford University Press, 1964), p. 605.

8. For two of the many discussions on "lucid intervals" by Victorian psychiatrists, see Burrows, *Commentaries*, p. 280, and John Haslam, *Observations on Madness and Melancholy* (1809; reprint, New York: Arno Press, 1976), pp. 46–47.

9. Lucretius uses similar apocalyptic imagery to describe the end of the world in the last book of *De rerum natura*.

10. Sigmund Freud, *The Interpretation of Dreams*, in *The Basic Writings of Sigmund Freud*, ed. A. A. Brill (New York: Modern Library, 1938), p. 356. According to Freud, "gaps" equal female genitalia with regard to dream symbolism.

11. Ibid., p. 357.

12. Christopher Ricks, *Tennyson* (New York: Macmillan, 1972), p. 290. Ricks believes the "juggernaut universe" was one of Tennyson's most important images of worldly chaos.

13. According to Freud in *The Interpretation of Dreams*, "one of these homologous dreams [i.e., of the same night] which comes first in time is usually the most distorted and most bashful, while the next dream is bolder and more distinct," *Basic Writings*, p. 357.

14. Lucretius, *De rerum natura*, p. 321.

15. Freud, *Totem and Taboo*, in *Basic Writings*, p. 863.

16. Erasmus Darwin is quoted by Hunter and Macalpine, *Three Hundred Years*, p. 548.

17. Christopher Ricks, *The Poems of Tennyson* (London: Longmans, Green, and Co., 1968), headnote, p. 1209.

18. James A. Freeman, "Tennyson, 'Lucretius,' and the 'Breasts of Helen,'" *Victorian Poetry* 11 (1973): 70.

19. Leonard M. Findlay, "Swinburne and Tennyson," *Victorian Poetry* 9 (1971): 232, examines the Venus in "Lucretius" as a "composite personality" of Venus Pandemos, the eroticized Venus that Lucretius rejects, and Venus Uranus, the genetrix that Lucretius adores.

20. Ricks, *The Poems of Tennyson*, p. 1213.

21. Henry Kozicki, *Tennyson and Clio: History in the Major Poems* (Baltimore: Johns Hopkins University Press, 1979), p. 157.

22. Ricks cites *Fasti* as the source of the Picus and Faunus myth in "Lucretius," *The Poems of Tennyson*, headnote, p. 1213.

23. The story of King Numa and Picus and Faunus is reprinted in Sir George Frazer, trans., *Ovid's Fasti* (Cambridge: Harvard University Press, 1951), pp. 143–45.

24. In Spenser's retelling of the tale, there is the mentioning of gelding as one of the possible punishments for Faunus's sexual crime.

25. David Shaw, *Tennyson's Style* (Ithaca: Cornell University Press, 1976), p. 109, believes that Tennyson employs "two-way syntax primarily to reveal a grammatically dissolving world" in which "the pursued is also the pursuer."

26. Ricks, *The Poems of Tennyson*, headnote, p. 1214.

27. Henry Maudsley, M.D. *Body and Mind . . . : To Which Are Added Psychological Essays* (New York: D. Appleton and Co., 1886), p. 28, uses the example of the "unclean spirit" and the will to show how the view of madness being caused by the "presence of an evil spirit" had "happily changed" in the Victorian period to a view that regarded derangement as "the result of nervous diseases, amenable to the same method of investigation as other nervous disorders" (p. 12).

28. Freud, *The Interpretation of Dreams*, in *Basic Writings*, p. 234.

29. Catherine Avery, *The New Classical Handbook* (New York: Appleton-Century-Crofts, 1962), pp. 649–50.

30. Ann C. Colley, *Tennyson and Madness* (Athens: University of Georgia Press, 1983), p. 90. I disagree with Colley that Lucretius goes mad because of his "unbridled passion," and that Tennyson uses madness in the poem to convey his "utter disgust at the power of the bestial nature to overthrow the noble Lucretius."

Chapter 5. "Rizpah"

1. Critics have generally viewed Rizpah as a paragon of grief and the poem as a criticism of social evils. Joshua Adler, "Tennyson's 'Mother of Sorrows': 'Rizpah,'" *Victorian Poetry* 12 (1974): 365, believes that Rizpah "anatomizes" the evils within her society and that her madness serves to make that criticism especially pointed. William E. Buckler, *The Victorian Imagination: Essays in Aesthetic Explorations* (New York: New York University Press, 1980), pp. 66–68, argues that Rizpah's madness "is not just a crippled state, but a heroic solution": in "Rizpah," "the efforts of the mad old woman to cope are notably successful through the evocation of a perseverance in a private myth" [about her son]. James Kincaid, *Tennyson's Major Poems: The Comic and Ironic Patterns* (New Haven: Yale University Press, 1975), p. 43, holds that "we must cast aside our social judgements and our social beings, it appears, in order to live with the elemental love and devotion of Rizpah." Paul Turner, *Tennyson* (London: Routledge and Kegan Paul, 1976), p. 174, also regards "Rizpah" as "a powerful protest against the type of religion that emphasized sin and punishment, rather than compassion, mercy, and long-suffering."

2. Jerome Hamilton Buckley, *Tennyson: The Growth of a Poet* (Cambridge: Harvard University Press, 1960), p. 218.

3. George O. Marshall, Jr., *A Tennyson Handbook* (New York: Twayne Publishers, 1963), p. 234. The penny magazine article recounts how the "Brighton Rizpah" nightly faced the stormiest elements to gather and bury the bones of her son Rooke, a man who was hanged in the latter part of the eighteenth century for robbing the mail. See also Hallam Tennyson, *Alfred Lord Tennyson: A Memoir by His Son* (New York: Greenwood Press, 1969), 2:249–51.

4. Marshall, *A Tennyson Handbook*, p. 187.

5. Adler, "Tennyson's Mother of Sorrows," p. 365. "There is no reference to madness in the original story on which the poem is based."

6. Adler, "Tennyson's Mother of Sorrows," p. 368.

7. Adler, "Tennyson's Mother of Sorrows," p. 364.

8. Kincaid, *Tennyson's Major Poems*, p. 143.

9. It has been widely documented in historical and psychiatric studies that the insane were treated like animals in the eighteenth century; they were beaten, considered bestial and demonic, and put on public exhibition. See Andrew T. Scull, ed., *Madhouses, Mad-Doctors, and Madmen: The Social History of Psychiatry in the Victorian Era* (Philadelphia: University of Pennsylvania Press, 1981), p. 108 and passim. See also Michel Foucault, *Madness and Civilization: A History of Insanity in the Age of Reason*, trans. Richard Howard (New York: Vintage Books, 1965), p. 70 and passim.

10. Sigmund Freud, *Mourning and Melancholia*, in James Strachey, ed., *The Standard Edition of the Complete Psychological Works of Sigmund Freud*, Vol. 14 (1914–1916) (London: The Hogarth Press, 1963), p. 249.

11. For a more detailed description of the mythical Great Mother, see J. C. Cooper, *An Illustrated Encyclopedia of Traditional Symbols* (London: Thames and Hudson, 1978), and the classic study, Erich Neumann, *The Great Mother: An Analysis of the Archetype*, trans. Ralph Mannheim (Princeton: Princeton University Press, 1974).

12. Neumann, *The Great Mother*, p. 71.

13. Freud, *Mourning and Melancholia*, p. 256.

14. Katherine Donnelly, *Recovering from the Loss of a Child* (New York: Macmillan, 1982), p. 42.

15. This compilation of theories on mourning by Freud, Abraham, and Melanie Klein can be found in Edith Weigert, *The Courage to Love* (New Haven: Yale University Press, 1970), p. 68.

16. Like "Rizpah," Poe's "Berenice" dramatizes the conflict between what Freud calls *eros* and *thanatos;* the teeth, like the bones, have a sexual component. Gothic elements in "Rizpah"—bones, stormy nights, wailing winds, and ghosts—make a comparison between Poe and Tennyson tempting, especially since Tennyson regarded Poe as "the most original American genius." Norman Page, *Tennyson: Interviews and Recollections* (Totowa, N.J.: Barnes and Noble, 1983), p. 6 n. 30.

17. Isaac Ray, *Contributions to Mental Pathology: A Facsimile Reproduction*, with an introduction by Jaques M. Quen (1828; reprint, New York: Scholars Facsimiles and Reprints, 1973), p. 488–89. In this early nineteenth-century psychiatric study, Ray discusses the development of early stages of insanity and its symptoms ("incubation") by focusing on *Hamlet* and *King Lear.* Like Shakespeare, Tennyson dramatizes characters who have a predisposition to madness, madness that manifests itself intermittently in mad speech and action.

18. For the fullest biographical treatment of Tennyson's and his family's experiences with depression, insanity, and mourning, see Robert Bernard Martin, *Tennyson: The Unquiet Heart* (Oxford: Clarendon Press, 1980), p. 20 and passim.

19. For an intriguing discussion of Victorian mourning rituals, see John Kucich, "Death Worship among the Victorians: *The Old Curiosity Shop*," *PMLA* 95 (1980): 58–73.

20. Reformed laws on capital punishment in Victorian England made petty crimes like theft no longer punishable by death or mutilation. As Scull documents, p. 6, in the realm of psychiatry, the Victorian age "saw the transformation of the madhouse into the asylum into the mental hospital; of the mad-doctor into the alienist into the psychiatrist; and of the madman (and madwoman) into the mental patient."

21. Kincaid, *Tennyson's Major Poems*, p. 144.

22. Freud, *Mourning and Melancholia*, p. 244.

23. Edith Weigert, *The Courage to Love* (New Haven: Yale University Press, 1970), p. 130.

24. According to Isaac Ray, *Contributions*, p. 504, before the Victorian period, Hamlet's "derangement was universally regarded as feigned." Because the Victorians had secularized religious visions into hallucinations, the possibility of considering the relationship between vision and hallucination, as in *Hamlet*, developed in studies of insanity.

Chapter 6. "Romney's Remorse"

1. Christopher Ricks, ed., *The Poems of Tennyson* (London: Longmans, Green, and Co., 1969), p. xxii. In his chronological table of Tennyson's life, Ricks records that in 1888 Tennyson suffered from "severe rheumatic illness, from which he does not recover till May 1889."

2. John R. Reed, *Victorian Conventions* (Athens: Ohio University Press, 1975), pp. 14–15, quotes Jeremy Taylor and discusses this popular Victorian belief in the moral design of illness. Reed describes other literary conventions—the woman as saint, the prodigal son, the deathbed scene—that are also present in "Romney's Remorse." For instance, like Dombey with Florence in the conclusion of *Dombey and Son* (or like Lear with Cordelia at the end of *King Lear*), Romney, a prodigal son, returns to his wife and is treated with unexpected kindness. At this point, Romney, like Dombey and Lear, realizes the merits of his discarded "pearl of great

price." But as I have tried to show in this paper, there are tensions in the poem that make Mary Abbot's status as a good nurse and Romney's as a Lear-like repentant sinner problematic.

3. See Ricks's note for "Romney's Remorse," *The Poems of Tennyson*, p. 1417, in which a reference is given to William Hayley's biography of George Romney.

4. See Arthur B. Chamberlain, *George Romney* (Freeport, N.Y.: Books for Libraries Press, 1971), p. 380. Chamberlain also reiterates that Romney was most famous for his paintings of mothers and children and for his portrait of King Lear being awakened by Cordelia, p. 29.

5. Philip Henderson, *Tennyson: Poet and Prophet* (London: Routledge and Kegal Paul, 1978), p. 196.

6. Harriet Taylor, "The Enfranchisement of Women" (1851; reprinted in *Essays on Sex Equality*, ed. Alice S. Rossi [Chicago: University of Chicago Press, 1951], pp. 107–16.

7. Catherine B. Stevenson, "Tennyson on Women's Rights," *Tennyson Research Bulletin*, November 1977, p. 27.

8. Stevenson, "Tennyson on Women's Rights," p. 23, quotes Tennyson as saying, "The blue coat school[s] have an income of £10,000 a year, this was left by founder for education of men and women equally. £150 only a year go for education of women. The member of Parliament does not make a stir about it because his constituents being male naturally do not want it altered. This kind of thing would be bettered by women's enfranchisement."

9. Diane Long Hoeveler, "Manly-Women and Womanly-Men: Tennyson's Androgynous Ideal in *The Princess* and *In Memoriam*," *Michigan Occasional Papers*, no. 19 (Spring 1981): 5–8.

10. Erasmus Darwin mentions this in *Zoonomia* (1796); he is quoted by Richard Hunter and Ida Macalpine in *Three Hundred Years of Psychiatry, 1535–1860: A History Presented in Selected English Texts* (London: Oxford University Press, 1964), p. 551.

11. Ricks, *The Poems of Tennyson*, traces the allusion to *Measure for Measure*, p. 1422.

12. Although very little has been written about "Romney's Remorse," there is a critical consensus that Mary is a highly admirable wife. George O. Marshall, *A Tennyson Handbook* (New York: Twayne Publishers, 1963), p. 234, reinstates Edward FitzGerald's belief (see Ricks, p. 1418) that " 'Mary's quiet act' " was " 'worth all Romney's pictures! even as a matter of Art, I am sure.' " But tensions within "Romney's Remorse" suggest that Tennyson was less sentimental about the relationship between Romney and Mary than the critics are.

Conclusion

1. Ann C. Colley, *Tennyson and Madness* (Athens: University of Georgia Press, 1983), p. 93.

2. William E. Fredeman, "One Word More—On Tennyson's Dramatic Monologues," in *Studies in Tennyson*, ed. Hallam Tennyson (London: Macmillan, 1981), p. 175.

3. Carol T. Christ, *Victorian and Modern Poetics* (Chicago: University of Chicago Press, 1984), p. 27.

4. Ibid., p. 48.

5. Elton Edward Smith, *The Two Voices: A Tennyson Study* (Lincoln: University of Nebraska Press, 1964), p. 1, uses this quotation from T. S. Eliot (in *Essays, Ancient*

and Modern) to support his theory that Tennyson's poetry reveals a divided sensibility.

6. For a discussion of how the critical climate influenced Tennyson's art, see Harold Nicolson, *Tennyson: Aspects of His Life Character and Poetry* (London: Constable, 1923), pp. 23–24.

7. James Knowles, "A Personal Reminiscence," in *Tennyson's Poetry: Authoritative Texts, Juvenila and Early Responses Criticism*, ed. Robert W. Hill, Jr. (New York: W. W. Norton, 1971), p. 581. See also Nicolson, *Tennyson*, pp. 111–20.

8. Cecil Y. Lang and Edgar F. Shannon, Jr., *The Letters of Alfred Lord Tennyson, Vol. 1, 1821–1850* (Cambridge, Mass.: Harvard University Press, Belknap Press, 1981), p. 264.

Bibliography

Abraham, Karl. *On Character and Libido Development: Six Essays.* New York: Basic Books, 1966.

Adler, Joshua. "Tennyson's 'Mother of Sorrows': 'Rizpah.'" *Victorian Poetry* 12 (1974): 363–69.

Allbright, Daniel. *Tennyson: The Muses' Tug-of-War.* Charlottesville: University Press of Virginia, 1986.

Allen, Matthew, M.D. *Cases of Insanity: With Medical, Moral, and Philosophical Observations and Essays upon Them.* Vol. 1, pt. 1. London: George Swire and H. Bellerby Publishers, 1831.

Armstrong, Isobel, ed. *The Major Victorian Poets: Reconsiderations.* Lincoln: University of Nebraska Press, 1969.

Auerbach, Nina. *Woman and the Demon: The Life of A Victorian Myth.* Cambridge: Harvard University Press, 1982.

Avery, Catherine. *The New Classical Handbook.* New York: Appleton-Century-Crofts, 1962.

Baker, Arthur E. *A Concordance to the Poetical and Dramatic Works of Alfred Lord Tennyson.* 1914; reprint, New York: Barnes and Noble, 1966.

Basham, Diana. "Tennyson and His Fathers: The Legacy of Manhood in Tennyson's Poems." *Tennyson Research Bulletin* 4 (November 1985): 163–78.

Basler, Roy P. *Sex, Symbolism, and Psychology in Literature.* New Brunswick: Rutgers University Press, 1948.

———. "Tennyson the Psychologist." *South Atlantic Quarterly* 43 (1944): 143–59.

Bennett, James R. "The Historical Abuse of Literature: Tennyson's 'Maud: A Monodrama' and the Crimean War." *English Studies* 66 (1981): 34–45.

Bersani, Leo. *Baudelaire and Freud.* Berkeley: University of California Press, 1977.

Brashear, William. *The Living Will: A Study of Tennyson and Nineteenth-Century Subjectivism.* Paris: Mouton, 1969.

Buckler, William E., ed. *Prose of the Victorian Period.* Boston: Houghton Mifflin Company, 1958.

———. "Tennysonian Madness: Mighty Collisions in the Imagination," in *The Victorian Imagination: Essays in Aesthetic Exploration,* edited by William E. Buckler, pp. 64–91. New York: New York University Press, 1980.

Buckley, Jerome Hamilton. *Tennyson: The Growth of a Poet.* Cambridge: Harvard University Press, 1960.

Bucknell, John Charles. *The Mad Folk of Shakespeare.* London: Macmillan, 1867.

Burrows, George Man. *Commentaries on the Causes, Forms, Symptoms, and Treatment, Moral and Medical, of Insanity.* 1828; reprint, New York: Arno Press, 1976.

Cary, M., et al., eds. *The Oxford Classical Dictionary.* Oxford: Clarendon Press, 1949.

Chamberlain, Arthur B. *George Romney.* Freeport, N.Y.: Books for Libraries Press, 1971.

Chandler, Alice. "Tennyson's *Maud* and the Song of Songs." *Victorian Poetry* 7 (1969): 91–104.

Christ, Carol T. *Victorian and Modern Poetics.* Chicago: University of Chicago Press, 1984.

Colley, Ann C. *Tennyson and Madness.* Athens: University of Georgia Press, 1983.

Cooper, J. C. *An Illustrated Encyclopedia of Traditional Symbols.* London: Thames and Hudson, 1978.

Coulson, John, ed. *The Saints: A Concise Biographical Dictionary.* New York: Hawthorn Books, 1958.

Culler, Dwight A. "Monodrama and the Dramatic Monologue." *PMLA* 90 (1975): 366–85.

———. *The Poetry of Tennyson.* New Haven: Yale University Press, 1977.

Delaney, John L., and James Edward Tobin, eds. *Dictionary of Catholic Biography.* New York: Doubleday, 1961.

Donnelly, Katherine. *Recovering from the Loss of a Child.* New York: Macmillan, 1982.

Dyson, Hope, and Charles Tennyson. *The Tennysons: Background to Genius.* London: Macmillan, 1974.

Ellenberger, Henri F. *The Discovery of the Unconscious.* New York: Basic Books, 1970.

Elliott, Phillip. "Tennyson and Spiritualism." *Tennyson Research Bulletin* 3 (November 1979): 89–100.

Findlay, Leonard M. "Swinburne and Tennyson." *Victorian Poetry* 9 (1971): 217–36.

Foucault, Michel. *Madness and Civilization: A History of Insanity in the Age of Reason.* Translated by Richard Howard. New York: Vintage Books, 1965.

———. *The History of Sexuality.* Vol. 1, *An Introduction.* Translated by Robert Hurley. New York: Random House, 1978.

Francis, Elizabeth, ed. *Tennyson: A Collection of Critical Essays.* Englewood Cliffs, N.J.: Prentice-Hall, 1980.

Fredeman, William E. " 'A Sign betwixt the Meadow and the Cloud': The Ironic Apotheosis of Tennyson's St. Simeon Stylites." *University of Toronto Quarterly* 38 (1968–69): 69–83.

———. "One Word More—On Tennyson's Dramatic Monologues." In *Studies in Tennyson,* edited by Hallam Tennyson. London; Macmillan, 1981.

Freeman, James A. "Tennyson, 'Lucretius' and the 'Breasts of Helen.' " *Victorian Poetry* 11 (1973): 69–75.

Freud, Sigmund. *Mourning and Melancholia.* In *The Standard Edition of the Complete Psychological Works of Sigmund Freud,* translated by James Strachey and Anna Freud and edited by James Strachey. Vol. 14 (1914–1916). London: Hogarth Press, 1963.

———. *The Interpretation of Dreams.* In *The Basic Writings of Sigmund Freud,* translated and edited by A. A. Brill. New York: Modern Library, 1938.

———. *Totem and Taboo.* In *The Standardized Edition of the Complete Psychological Works of Sigmund Freud,* translated by James Strachey and Anna Freud and edited by James Strachey. Vol. 13 (1912–13). London: Hogarth Press, 1963.

Gay, Peter. *Education of the Senses: Victoria to Freud.* New York: Oxford University Press, 1984.

Giordano, Frank, Jr. "The 'Red-Ribbed Hollow,' Suicide and Part III in 'Maud.'" *Notes and Queries* 24 (1977): 402–4.

Harrison, Brian. "Underneath the Victorians." *Victorian Studies* 10 (1967): 239–62.

Haslam, John. *Observations on Madness and Melancholy.* 1809; reprint, New York: Arno Press, 1976.

Hellstrom, Ward. *On the Poems of Tennyson.* Gainesville: University of Florida Press, 1972.

Henderson, Philip. *Tennyson: Poet and Prophet.* London: Routledge and Kegan Paul, 1978.

Hone, William. *The Everyday Book; or, A Guide to the Year.* Vol. 1. London: William Tegg, 1878.

Hunter, Richard, and Ida Macalpine. *Three Hundred Years of Psychiatry, 1535–1860: A History Presented in Selected English Texts.* London: Oxford University Press, 1964.

Jay, Elizabeth. *The Religion of the Heart: Anglican Evangelism in the Nineteenth-Century Novel.* Oxford: Clarendon Press, 1979.

Jenkyns, Richard. *The Victorians and Ancient Greece.* Cambridge: Harvard University Press, 1980.

Johnson, E. D. H. *The Alien Vision of Victorian Poetry: Sources of Poetic Imagination in Tennyson, Browning, and Arnold.* 1952; reprint, Hamdon, Conn.: Archon Books, 1963.

———. "The Lily and the Rose: Symbolic Meaning in Tennyson's *Maud.*" *PMLA* 64 (1949): 1222–27.

Joseph, Gerhard. *Tennysonian Love: The Strange Diagonal.* Minneapolis: University of Minnesota Press, 1969.

Kendall, J. K. "Gem Imagery in Tennyson's 'Maud.'" *Victorian Poetry* 17 (1979): 389–94.

Kennedy, Ian H. C. "The Crisis of Language in Tennyson's *Maud.*" *Texas Studies in Literature and Language* 19 (1977): 161–78.

Killham, John. "Tennyson's 'Maud'—The Function of the Imagery." In *Critical Essays on the Poetry of Tennyson,* edited by John Killham, pp. 219–35. London: Routledge and Kegan Paul, 1960.

Kincaid, James R. *Tennyson's Major Poems: The Comic and Ironic Patterns.* New Haven: Yale University Press, 1975.

Kissane, James. *Alfred Tennyson.* New York: Twayne Publishers, 1970.

Kozicki, Henry. *Tennyson and Clio: History in the Major Poems.* Baltimore: Johns Hopkins University Press, 1979.

Kübler-Ross, Elisabeth. *On Death and Dying.* New York: Macmillan Publishing Co., 1969.

Kucich, John. "Death Worship among the Victorians: *The Old Curiosity Shop.*" *PMLA* 95 (1980): 58–73.

Laing, R. D. *Self and Others.* New York: Pantheon Books, 1969.

———. *The Divided Self.* New York: Pantheon Books, 1969.

Lang, Cecil Y., and Edgar F. Shannon, Jr., eds. *The Letters of Alfred Lord Tennyson. Vol. 1, 1821–1850.* Cambridge: Harvard University Press, Belknap Press, 1981.

Langbaum, Robert. *The Poetry of Experience: The Dramatic Monologue in Modern Literary Tradition.* London: Chatto and Windus, 1957.

Levine, George. *The Boundaries of Fiction.* Princeton: Princeton University Press, 1968.

Lewis, Helen B. *Shame and Guilt in Neurosis.* New York: International Universities Press, 1971.

Lucretius. *De rerum natura.* Translated by W. H. D. Rouse. Revised with new text, introduction, notes and index by Martin Ferguson Smith. Cambridge; Harvard University Press, 1975.

Marcus, Stephen. *The Other Victorians: A Study of Sexuality and Pornography in Mid-Nineteenth Century England.* New York: Basic Books, 1966.

Marshall, George O. *A Tennyson Handbook.* New York: Twayne Publishers, 1963.

Martin, Robert Bernard. *Tennyson: The Unquiet Heart.* Oxford: Clarendon Press, 1980.

Maudsley, Henry, M.D. *Body and Will: Being an Essay Concerning Will in its Metaphysical, Physiological, and Pathological Aspects.* New York: D. Appleton and Co., 1884.

————. *The Pathology of Mind: A Study of Distempers, Deformities, and Disorders.* 2d ed. 1895; reprint, London: Julian Friedmann Publishers, 1979.

Mermin, Dorothy. *The Audience in the Poem: Five Victorian Poets.* New Brunswick, N.J.: Rutgers University Press, 1983.

Miyoshi, Masao. *The Divided Self: A Perspective on the Literature of the Victorians.* New York: New York University Press, 1969.

Nicolson, Harold. *Tennyson: Aspects of His Life Character and Poetry.* London: Constable, 1923.

Ostriker, Alicia. "The Three Modes in Tennyson's Prosody." *PMLA* 82 (1967): 273–84.

Ovid. *Fasti.* Translated by Sir George Frazer. Cambridge: Harvard University Press, 1951.

Pinel, Philippe. *A Treatise on Insanity.* Translated by D. D. Davis, M.D. 1806; reprint, New York: Hafner Publishing Co., 1962.

Priestley, F. E. L. *Language and Structure in Tennyson's Poetry.* London: André Deutsch, 1975.

Rader, Ralph Wilson. *Tennyson's Maud: The Biographical Genesis.* Berkeley: University of California Press, 1963.

Reed, John R. *Victorian Conventions.* Athens: Ohio University Press, 1975.

Richardson, Joanna. *The Pre-Eminent Victorian: A Study of Tennyson.* London: Jonathan Cape, 1962.

Ricks, Christopher. *Tennyson.* New York: Collier Books, 1972.

————, ed. *The Poems of Tennyson.* London: Longmans, Green and Co., 1969.

Rosen, George. *Madness in Society: Chapters in the Historical Sociology of Mental Illness.* Chicago: University of Chicago Press, 1969.

Rycroft, Charles. *A Critical Dictionary of Psychoanalysis.* Totowa, N.J.: Littlefield, Adams and Co., 1973.

Scott, Patrick Gregg. " 'Flowering in a Lonely World': Tennyson and the Victorian Study of Language." *Victorian Poetry* 18 (1980): 371–81.

Scull, Andrew T. ed. *Madhouses, Mad-Doctors, and Madmen: The Social History of*

Psychiatry in the Victorian Era. Philadelphia: University of Pennsylvania Press, 1981.

Shannon, Edgar J. "The Critical Reception of Tennyson's 'Maud.'" *PMLA* 68 (1953): 397–417.

Shaw, David W. "Imagination and Intellect in Tennyson's 'Lucretius.'" *Modern Language Quarterly* 32 (1972): 130–39.

———. *Tennyson's Style.* Ithaca: Cornell University Press, 1976.

Showalter, Elaine, and English Showalter. "Victorian Women and Menstruation." *Victorian Studies* 14 (1970–71): 83–89.

Skultans, Vieda. *Madness and Morals: Ideas on Insanity in the Nineteenth Century.* London: Routledge and Kegan Paul, 1975.

Smith, Edward Elton. *The Two Voices: A Tennyson Study.* Lincoln: University of Nebraska Press, 1964.

Spatz, Jonas. "Love and Death in Tennyson's *Maud. Texas Studies in Literature and Language* 16 (1974–75): 503–10.

Swanson, David W., M.D.; Philip J. Bohnert, M.D.; and Jackson A. Smith, M.D. *The Paranoid.* Boston: Little, Brown and Co., 1970.

Taylor, Harriet. "The Enfranchisement of Women." 1851; reprinted in *Essays on Sex Equality,* edited by Alice S. Rossi. Chicago: University of Chicago Press, 1951.

Tennyson, Charles. *Alfred Tennyson.* New York: Macmillan Co., 1949.

Tennyson, Hallam. *Alfred Lord Tennyson: A Memoir by His Son.* 2 vols. London: Macmillan Co., 1898. Reprint. New York: Greenwood Press, 1969.

Timko, Michael. "The Victorianism of Victorian Literature." *New Literary History* 6 (1974–75): 607–27.

Tucker, Herbert F., Jr. "From Monomania to Monologue: 'St. Simeon Stylites' and the Rise of the Victorian Monologue." *Victorian Poetry* 22 (1984): 121–37.

Turner, Paul. *Tennyson.* London: Routledge and Kegan Paul, 1976.

Veith, Ilza. *Hysteria: The History of the Disease.* Chicago: University of Chicago Press, 1965.

Weigert, Edith. *The Courage to Love.* New Haven: Yale University Press, 1970.

Weiner, Ronald. "The Chord of Self: Tennyson's *Maud.*" *Psychology and Literature* 16 (1966): 175–83.

Wilner, Ortha. "Tennyson and Lucretius." *Classical Journal* 25 (1930): 347–66.

Wordsworth, Jonathan. "Double Meaning: III, 'What is it has been done?': The Central Problem of *Maud.*" *Essays in Criticism* 24 (1974): 356–62.

Index